Dignity for All

Dignity for All
How to Create a World Without Rankism

Robert W. Fuller and Pamela A. Gerloff

Berrett–Koehler Publishers, Inc.
San Francisco
a BK Currents book

Berrett-Koehler Publishers, Inc.
235 Montgomery Street, Suite 650
San Francisco, California 94104-2916
Tel: (415) 288-0260, Fax: (415) 362-2512
www.bkconnection.com

Ordering information for print editions

Quantity sales. Special discounts are available on quantity purchases by corporations,
associations, and others. For details, contact the "Special Sales Department" at the Berrett-
Koehler address above.

Individual sales. Berrett-Koehler publications are available through most bookstores. They
can also be ordered directly from Berrett-Koehler: Tel: (800) 929-2929; Fax: (802) 864-7626;
www.bkconnection.com

Orders for college textbook/course adoption use. Please contact Berrett-Koehler:
Tel: (800) 929-2929; Fax: (802) 864-7626.

Orders by U.S. trade bookstores and wholesalers. Please contact Ingram Publisher Services, Tel:
(800) 509-4887; Fax: (800) 838-1149; E-mail: customer.service@ingrampublisherservices.com;
or visit www.ingrampublisherservices.com/Ordering for details about electronic ordering.

Berrett-Koehler and the BK logo are registered trademarks of Berrett-Koehler Publishers, Inc.

First Edition
Paperback print edition ISBN 978-1-57675-789-5
PDF e-book ISBN 978-1-57675-770-3
2008-1

Contents

List of Sidebars

Acknowledgments

This book owes its existence to the wisdom and perseverance of dignitarians past and present, who daily set an example for those around them; and to the current generation of young people, who inspire us to live our way into the vision of a world without rankism.

We also wish to acknowledge and thank the following individuals:

Ruth Ann Harnisch, president of the Harnisch Family Foundation, for her early, visionary support of Robert Fuller's work on dignity and rankism. Her creative ideas, commitment, and passionate philanthropy helped to boldly spread the word about rankism and the need to build a dignitarian world. She also provided valuable counsel to this project at various stages;

Adam Fuller, for helping to define the intent and scope of this project at the outset;

Joyce Gibson, for her powerful application of the dignity work, her unwavering support, and insightful commentary;

Joyce Hempstead, our book designer, for her skill, patience, and good humor;

Jan Hooker-Haring, for her discerning editorial eye;

John Beck, Paul Birnie, Noah Brand, Benjamin Fuller, Karen Fuller, Brian Gerloff, Nancy Haerter, Jeannie Norris, Jennifer Prost, Steve Renne, Carol Soderholm, Kathleen Spaltro, and Elizabeth Tobin, for their thoughtful comments on earlier versions of the manuscript and their insights and support for this project;

Wendy Anderson, Wendy Angus, Marianna Cacciatore, Deborah Dunham, Lillian Greeley, Vern Hunter, Christopher Mogil, Cathy Tell, Mary Terhune, and Ralph Tucker for their helpful input;

All those who provided supporting materials, such as anecdotes, quotations, resources, and appended material;

Elisa Cooper and Diane Castigliani, for their technical expertise and cheerful assistance with the dignity websites;

Stephanie Heuer, for making dignity rock for children and teenagers (see www.dignityrocks.com), and Suze Rutherford and Kim Holl, for also taking the dignity work to schools and young people;

Mara Peluso, for her enthusiastic support, editorial comments, and creative suggestions to improve all aspects of the book;

Lisa Gerloff-Banker, for her extensive feedback and sound editorial advice;

Robert Gerloff, for his comments on the manuscript and for truly championing the dignity work;

John Steiner, for his ongoing and invaluable support as connector, editor, and ally;

Claire Sheridan and Jane Gerloff, whose extensive and varied contributions have, as always, been indispensable;

Johanna Vondeling, Jeevan Sivasubramaniam, Dianne Platner, Debra Gates, and Berrett-Koehler Publishers, for their professionalism and their commitment to living by dignitarian values.

Insofar as *Dignity for All* draws on earlier works, we thank as well the many contributors acknowledged in Robert Fuller's books *Somebodies and Nobodies* and *All Rise*.

–Robert W. Fuller and Pamela A. Gerloff

chapter one

Dignity: What Everybody Really Wants

Dignity. Isn't that what everybody really wants? You, me, your parents, your children, your friends, your colleagues at work: All of us want to be treated with dignity.

The homeless person in the park; the elderly in nursing homes; students, teachers, principals; Christians, Jews, Muslims; taxi drivers, store clerks, waiters, police officers; prisoners and guards; immigrants; doctors, patients, nurses; the poor, the wealthy, the middle class; big nations, small nations, people without a homeland.

Dignity. Everybody wants it, craves it, seeks it. People's whole lives change when they're treated with dignity—and when they're not.

Evan Ramsey, now serving a 210-year prison sentence for shooting and killing his high school principal and another student in Bethel, Alaska, told criminologist Susan Magestro:

"I was picked on seven hours a day every day and the teachers didn't do anything to help me…I told [my foster mother] and [my principal] more than a dozen times about all the bullying I was subjected to. They never did anything to help me.…If I can prevent someone from having the experience I went through, I want to do that. I killed people.… Don't respond with violence even if you're provoked. There's no hope for me now but there is hope for you."

—From "The Realities and Issues Facing Juveniles and Their Families,
The Warning Signs: Evan Ramsey—Bethel, Alaska,"
by Susan Magestro, www.susanmagestro.com

Fundamentally, dignity is about respect and value. It means treating yourself and others with respect just because you're alive on the planet. It's recognizing that you and everyone else have a right to be here, and that you belong. It means valuing your own and others' presence and special qualities. It means honoring who you are and what you have to offer. It means creating a culture in which it is safe for everyone to contribute their own gifts and talents.

Dignity. It's a need so strong that people will give up their freedom to have it met; an inner drive so insistent that it can move people to shocking acts of revenge when the attempt to achieve it is thwarted; a human value so critical to happiness and well-being that people sometimes value it more than life itself.

A Human Need Ignored

Yet this craving for dignity is so commonly overlooked that most of us accept undignified treatment as "just the way it is." As victims, we may wince inwardly, but we bite our tongues ("Who am I to protest?" "What good will it do?"). As perpetrators, we excuse our behavior ("I'm the boss, aren't I?" "He deserved it." "I'm just evening the score."). Or we ignore our nagging conscience, failing to acknowledge, even to ourselves, that we are violating another's dignity.

Every day, we witness dignity scorned in our personal relationships, families, businesses, schools, healthcare facilities, religious institutions, and governmental bodies. Routinely, we fail to accord dignity to those we perceive to be the weaker among us. They may be the old, the young, the poor, the unknown, the infirm, the female, the darker colored, the jobless, the less skilled, or the less attractive.

Yet experiencing indignity at the hands of others is not limited to those at the bottom of the hierarchy—as the wealthy, the famous, and the beautiful will attest. Anywhere and everywhere dignity is transgressed by others, with surprising regularity: A supervisor harasses an employee. A child taunts a classmate. A sports team hazes new members. A customer speaks rudely to a waitress. A teacher gives preferential treatment to a friend's child. An adult verbally abuses a child. An administrator fires a whistle-blower. A government official secretly circumvents the law. A prison guard torments an inmate. A dictator steals from the national treasury. A superpower pressures a smaller nation to commit to a loan that will damage its economy.

From intimate relationships to global relations, indignity is commonplace. Think of your own experiences: when have *you* not been treated with dignity? When have you failed to treat others with dignity?

So Why Are We Surprised?

If, every day, so many of us are not treated with the health-giving, life-affirming dignity we crave, then why are we so shocked when an employee "goes postal," a teenager goes on a violent rampage, a mild-mannered woman explodes in anger at a seemingly small provocation, or global tensions escalate into international crises? Why do we habitually fail to recognize, beneath the violent outbursts, the powerful impulse to lash out when a fundamental birthright has been denied: the right to be treated with dignity?

"The sense that you are nothing or nobody can drive you to violence and unreason. Through all human history it has been the hidden motive— that unbearable desire to prove oneself somebody—behind countless insanities and acts of violence."

—John Fowles, author of *The French Lieutenant's Woman*

A Price to Pay

Of course, acts of revenge are never justified. But we ignore at great cost to ourselves and society the fundamental urge to be treated with dignity.

The consequences of violating others' dignity are evident: in widespread social problems such as high rates of school dropout, prison incarceration, violent crime, depression, suicide, divorce, and despair; in the business world in reduced creativity, lower productivity, or disloyalty to the organization. Even health and longevity are affected.

Dignity Not Yet Won

In 1775, American patriot Patrick Henry boldly declared, "Give me liberty or give me death!" Americans won their freedom, but more than two centuries later have not yet secured their dignity; nor has the rest of the world.

But that may be changing.

Today, the age-old cry for liberty appears to be morphing into a heartfelt cry for dignity. Worldwide, we see dignity-denying dictatorships transforming into democracies. In democratic elections, we see growing voter enthusiasm for candidates who offer a vision of dignity for all. If we look carefully, we can see in terrorist assaults the craving to be treated with dignity; and the spate of school shootings in recent years has led adults to counteract the devastating effects of bullying among children through school-sponsored anti-bullying programs. As overwhelming as the problem of indignity may seem, historically, humans have grown more tolerant and respectful as a species than we once were. Equal rights protections for people of different genders, skin colors, physical abilities, and sexual orientations are just some examples of progress toward greater dignity for all.

The time is ripe for dignity.

We Can Lead the Way

Each of us plays many different roles in life: we are parents, relatives, friends; we are employers and employees; we are participants in religious, school, or municipal governing bodies; we are citizens of the world in a community of nations. In each of these roles, we yearn to be treated with dignity, and in each of these roles, we have the opportunity to show what it looks and feels like to give dignified treatment to others.

We can begin to create a "dignitarian" world by simply asking ourselves: How can I help create a culture of dignity wherever I am?

- If we hope to ever live in peace with one another;
- if we wish to live in a world where people of differing opinions and

beliefs, differing experiences and cultures, differing languages, lifestyles, expectations, and aspirations can co-exist in harmony;

- if we aspire to realize the potential of our young people, our senior citizens, our work force, our political leadership;

- if we aim to harness the resources of talent, purpose, creativity, and joy lying right at our fingertips;

- if we dream of finding creative, life-affirming solutions to age-old problems,

then together, let us take the first step. Let us begin to acknowledge and respect the innate human yearning for dignity.

Let each of us lead the way.

Dignity as a Universal Right

This book is a beginning: it is a primer, a handbook, a manifesto. It aims to outline a pathway into a bold new world—a world where dignity is the norm, the natural and expected way of being; a world where violations of dignity are regarded as unacceptable; a world where, in the words of Vartan Gregorian, president of the Carnegie Corporation of New York, "Dignity is not negotiable." Since dignity is a basic human need, dignity in a "dignitarian society" will be treated as both a human right and a responsibility. Dignified treatment will be just the way it is.

> *"Dignity is not negotiable."*
>
> —Vartan Gregorian, president of the Carnegie Corporation of New York

A Dignitarian World Emerging

What would such a world look like? What would home and family, school, work, religious, medical, social, political, environmental, and governmental life look like, sound like, feel like? How can we create such a vision? What steps can we take to get there?

Dignity for All provides a roadmap for a dignitarian world emerging. It is an invitation to journey to a new and tantalizing land, where a society that truly lives the value of dignity for all no longer asks the question "Could such a world be possible?" The question asked instead is "How soon can we make it happen?"

KEY POINTS

- Dignity is a basic human need. Therefore everyone has a right to be treated with dignity.

- People routinely violate others' dignity, in large and small ways, throughout the world.

- When people's dignity is not respected, negative feelings and unhealthy consequences result, for individuals and society.

- If we want to achieve our potential, we must make dignity a primary value.

- Each of us can help build a dignitarian world.

Small Acts: The Power of "I'm Sorry"

"I was waiting in line. A young guy about 20 was at the counter buying stamps. Suddenly some ratty, crazed-looking man who was ahead of me in line started screaming obscenities at the young guy. Young Guy turned around and said, 'What? What did I do?' to the livid man, who screamed back, 'You KNOW what you're doing!' like he was sensing evil rays coming out of Young Guy's forehead or something.

Young Guy kept saying 'What?' and then he just stood there. Everyone in the room froze up. It was extremely tense. Then Young Guy, in an apparent moment of inspiration, said simply to the crazed man, 'I'm sorry, I didn't mean to disrespect you.'

That comment was like a pin deflating the man's anger. He completely calmed down and backed off, because he felt he had his dignity back."

—Claire S.

chapter two

Naming the Problem

"At the core of every humiliation and indignity is a mental error, not just a habit… Nothing can be done until it is noticed, until it is named. Naming creates distinctions, distinctions create the capacity to change. Naming rankism transforms everything."

—Paul Hawken, author of *Natural Capitalism*

Humans have been violating others' dignity for millennia. We have raped and pillaged, trafficked in slavery, and otherwise abused our fellow creatures. Colonialism; segregation; apartheid; torture; ethnic cleansing; corporate corruption; monopolistic pricing; sexual harassment; discrimination based on race, gender, age, appearance… The list of ways we have violated the dignity of members of our own and other species goes on and on.

So why would we think we can stop it now?

The reasons are simple:

- *We have already made progress in this area as a species.*
  As bad as things may sometimes seem, in much of the world we now have laws that disallow such behavior. Compared to the

world of even a few hundred years ago, modern humanity does
have a few things going for it when it comes to dignity.

- *A "right idea" at the "right time" with the "right tools" to make it a reality can change the world.* **And we now have a new idea and new tools to stop indignity.**

Think of the invention of the airplane and the state of commercial
flight today, or the manufacture of the first telephone and the complexity of global communications now, or the progress made in
the United States toward equal rights for women since the 1960's.
When a new idea is introduced into the collective consciousness of
a people along with the tools to make it easily accessible to many,
that new idea or phenomenon has a decent chance of taking hold.

In this book we'll be introducing a word that has recently
entered our language—a new "tool" that allows us to address
with unprecedented effectiveness the age-old tendency of
humanity to infringe on others' dignity. We also have new mass
communication tools, as well as experience with non-violent
social movements to uplift humanity. Which is to say, we now
have the right tools at our disposal and enough experience as a
species to really change the world.

The Crucial Tool: A Single Word

In 1963, Betty Friedan characterized the plight of women as "the problem
that has no name." Within a few years, the problem had acquired one:
sexism. Only after naming the source of gender inequality did the
movement to disallow gender-based discrimination grab hold of the collective consciousness. Once named, the problem was identifiable, visible,
discussable—and actionable. And, ultimately, it became preventable.

Rankism: Abuse of the Power Attached to Rank

The word for the source of dignity violation is rankism. *Rankism is abuse
of the power attached to rank.* When a boss shouts at an employee, that's
rankism. When a doctor demeans a nurse, that's rankism. When a cus-

tomer is rude to a waitress, that's rankism. When a professor exploits a graduate student, that's rankism. When a company executive has an intimate relationship with an intern and she loses her job over it, but he doesn't, that's rankism.

On a societal scale, rankism may take the form of political and corporate corruption, sexual abuse by clergy, maltreatment of elders in nursing homes, humiliation of prisoners by guards, large nations intimidating smaller nations into serving the larger country's interests, or genocide. In short, rankism is when those of higher rank, i.e., those with power over another, treat those of lower rank in ways that violate their dignity.

The Power of Naming

To have a name is to be.

—Benoît Mandelbrot

Once the word *rankism* had been coined, people started talking about it on a website devoted to identifying and disallowing it. [*See www.dignityforall.org.*] Here are some of their comments:

- "Rankism gives a name to something we've all experienced but probably not given much thought to. Once you have a name for it, you see it everywhere."
- "Recognizing rankism makes you more conscious of your dignity."
- "Rankism is so ingrained, so common, that it's hard to even notice it."
- "I have begun using the term rankism, explained it to my friends, and now they are using it, too."

Sometimes rankism is unconscious; a simple, unwitting misuse of power. But often, the misuse of power occurs because the perpetrator feels "special" or "better than" someone else and believes that this position of superiority carries with it license to diminish the other person's dignity. Common, everyday snobbery falls into this category, as do racism, sexism, classism, and other "isms." Feeling superior to others for any reason usually gives rise to rankism.

The Root of All "Isms"

The word *rankism* gets at the heart of what all the other "isms" in our
lives are about. Rankism is an umbrella term that encompasses racism,
sexism, classism, ageism, and any other ism that sets one group or
individual apart from another and then claims superiority. These more
specific "isms" are subspecies of
rankism. With all "isms," one person or group believes itself to be
"better than" another, and uses
its perceived rank to deprive
others of their dignity.

*"Rankism is the 'ism' that, once
eradicated, would pretty much
eliminate the rest of them."*

—from www.dignityforall.org

> **Rankism: A Concept that Both Progressives and Conservatives Can Love**
>
> The concept of rankism is indispensable for progressives and conservatives alike. It
> enables us to resolve a confusing core issue central to both society and our personal
> lives—hierarchy vs. equality. For decades, our value of equality in relationships and
> desire for "flatter" organizational structures has been challenged by our daily experi-
> ence of rank and hierarchy, such as the natural hierarchies of parent-child, staff-volun-
> teers in nonprofit groups. The concept of rankism gives us a way to distinguish between
> appropriate ranking and the abuse of rank (rankism) and set aside the latter in our
> personal relationships, our organizations, and our international relations.
>
> —Bill Moyer, author of *Doing Democracy*

Objections Raised

Some people, upon hearing the word rankism, reflexively exclaim, "We
don't need *another* 'ism!'" That's understandable, given the proliferation
of "isms" and the fact that they have sometimes been used to label or
attack others. But what if, as explained above, this "ism" is not in competi-
tion with the others, but instead encompasses all of them? Rankism may
well be the overarching "ism" that finally allows us to liberate ourselves
from the entire range of specific problems the other "isms" describe.

Some people at first object to the concept of rankism because they fear it may undermine progress in eradicating other forms of social prejudice. But rankism need not undermine any of the groundbreaking, often painstaking, work that so many are doing on behalf of those who suffer discrimination of particular kinds. Instead, the concept of rankism can be a powerful tool to help solidify gains humanity has already made in those areas, while simultaneously helping to make dignity for all a new standard for the human species.

> **Question for Contemplation:**
> When have you felt "better than" someone else? Has that feeling of superiority ever led you to treat someone with less dignity than you would want to be treated?

Why the Concept of Rankism Is Important

The concept of rankism is important because it allows us to change attitudes and behaviors that cause suffering—in ourselves and in society .

Suffering occurs in the world, with or without rankism, but rankism produces unnecessary and avoidable suffering. Starving children suffer, but they suffer needlessly when corrupt government officials divert food shipments to the children in exchange for cash for their own personal gain. A school child may feel hurt by a classmate's inadvertent slight, but greater suffering is inflicted when one child deliberately bullies another and nothing is done about it. Teenagers grapple with the challenges of entering adulthood, but their struggles become all the more painful when other teens ridicule, ostracize, or demand conformity to group norms.

Rankism causes suffering, and rankism can be stopped.

What is Dignity?

Dignity is not always easy to define, but it's easy to detect. We know it when we see it, and when we experience it. Dignity involves respect—respect for oneself and for others. It also has to do with worthiness—a sense that we and others are worthy. While it is true that we can maintain our dignity even when others treat us with indignity, treating ourselves and others with dignity means treating everyone as if they matter and are worthy of our respect.

Dignity can also involve recognizing our right to belong. In this sense, dignity is knowing there's a place for us. Then dignity and recognition are two sides of a coin. Dignity is the sense of belonging, of inclusion, of being valued, that comes when we know that we have contributed something of ourselves to a group and that our place in it is secure. We experience dignity and belonging as threats of exclusion and banishment are removed.

The Relationship of Dignity to Rankism

Like other abstract nouns (for example, liberty and justice), dignity is sometimes more easily understood in the negative. Everyone has felt the sting of indignity. We're fine-tuned to detect it—even in small gestures, like an eyebrow arched in disdain—precisely because such signals are precursors of rejection. Not so long ago banishment meant death.

Indignity results not from rank differences per se, but rather from abuses of rank. We call these abuses of power "rankism." Indignities are due to rankism; rankism results in indignity.

Creating a Culture of Dignity

We establish a culture of dignity by disallowing indignity—which means disallowing rankism. In the same way that we build a multicultural society as we overcome racism, we build a dignitarian society as we overcome rankism.

A dignitarian society does not make everyone equal in rank, but rather disallows rankism, thereby making everyone equal in dignity, regardless of their rank.

The Golden Rule—Do unto others as you would have others do unto you—is a precept found in many religious and philosophical systems. It is an operating principle for a dignitarian society. As we treat others with the dignity we ourselves desire and deserve, we create a culture of dignity.   (continued)

Implications of Creating a Dignitarian Society

Not only is the principle of equal dignity for all fair and just, it also results in greater creativity, productivity, health, and happiness. In short, dignitarian organizations and societies gain a competitive edge.

Like love, dignity can best take hold in the absence of abuse and discrimination, exploitation, and predation. But once dignity is secure, it can help carry us from liberty to the justice that still eludes many democratic societies.

KEY POINTS:

- It's now possible for humanity to take a giant step toward creating a dignitarian world because we have new tools.

- These tools include (1) a new word—*rankism*—and (2) mass communication systems that allow ideas to spread quickly.

- Rankism is abuse of the power attached to rank. It is the "ism" that underlies all other "isms," such as racism and sexism.

- The concept of rankism is useful because it identifies the cause of so much unnecessary suffering in the world.

- Once rankism has been identified, we can take concrete steps to prevent it.

chapter three

Naming the Solution

et's face it. Humans are predatory animals. Throughout history, the stronger or more powerful members of our species have preyed upon the weaker among us. Because this predatory—i.e., rankist—behavior has such deep historical roots, it can be hard to imagine a world that has rank without rankism. It can be hard to envision a world where rank holders use their rank to protect the dignity of all.

But we *can* begin to imagine such a world. In fact, moving beyond our predatory instincts may well be the only sane course of action if we want to have a chance at species survival. We live today in a world with massive societal challenges—poverty, famine, crime, disease, climate change, and war. We possess weaponry that cannot be reliably confined or controlled. As rankism begets further rankism, cycles of rankism escalate. If ever we are to free ourselves from retaliatory rankist behavior, we will need to disallow rankism, and instead create cultures of dignity.

It's a daunting task, but not impossible. Time and again, humans have shown that we can choose a worthy goal and accomplish it. *The end of apartheid in South Africa, segregation in America, and the tyrannies of communism in formerly Iron Curtain countries are the result of movements that began with a vision of dignity for all and accomplished significant dignitarian goals.*

Moreover, humans have demonstrated that we have the capacity to interrupt the cycle of rankism [*See Diagrams 1 and 2*], by choosing to respond to indignity in a dignitarian way. An outstanding example is when Nelson Mandela came to power as president of South Africa after spending 27 years as a political prisoner. The new government he headed chose to pursue a path of peace and reconciliation, rather than revenge, for the brutalities committed under apartheid.

Dignity Works

Rank without rankism is a new social construct. It carries with it the understanding that rank in itself is not the problem; rankism is the problem. Rank can be used to protect human dignity, not debase it. Rank can be used to bring order, harmony, and efficiency to the accomplishment of worthy goals. Rank can be used to benefit others, not to serve our own egos or enrich ourselves at the expense of others. In fact,

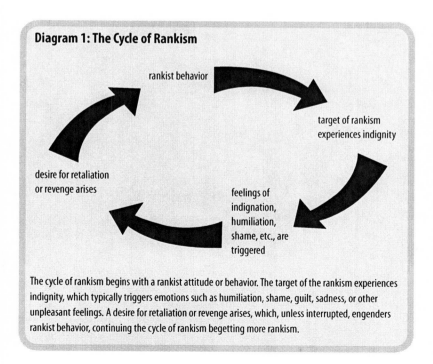

Diagram 1: The Cycle of Rankism

rankist behavior

target of rankism experiences indignity

feelings of indignation, humiliation, shame, etc., are triggered

desire for retaliation or revenge arises

The cycle of rankism begins with a rankist attitude or behavior. The target of the rankism experiences indignity, which typically triggers emotions such as humiliation, shame, guilt, sadness, or other unpleasant feelings. A desire for retaliation or revenge arises, which, unless interrupted, engenders rankist behavior, continuing the cycle of rankism begetting more rankism.

rank is often useful, even essential, to get things done. Rank can even be helpful for ending rankism. It is much easier, for example, to raise standards of behavior within an organization when a person of high rank helps establish and enforce practices that preserve dignity for all than when those of lower rank must risk being fired for trying to create such changes on their own.

As we envision a world of rank without rankism, we lay the groundwork for a dignitarian world to become reality. And then a hidden truth reveals itself: dignity works. Dignity produces not only more effective

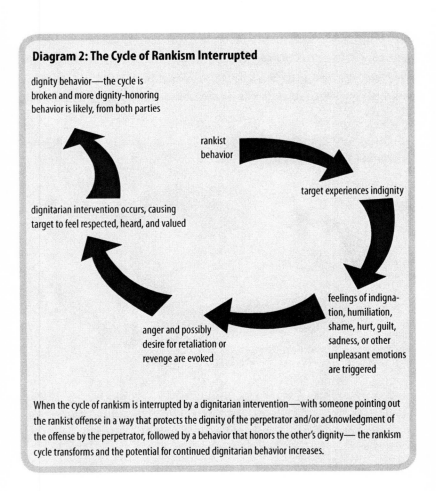

Diagram 2: The Cycle of Rankism Interrupted

dignity behavior—the cycle is broken and more dignity-honoring behavior is likely, from both parties

rankist behavior

target experiences indignity

dignitarian intervention occurs, causing target to feel respected, heard, and valued

anger and possibly desire for retaliation or revenge are evoked

feelings of indignation, humiliation, shame, hurt, guilt, sadness, or other unpleasant emotions are triggered

When the cycle of rankism is interrupted by a dignitarian intervention—with someone pointing out the rankist offense in a way that protects the dignity of the perpetrator and/or acknowledgment of the offense by the perpetrator, followed by a behavior that honors the other's dignity— the rankism cycle transforms and the potential for continued dignitarian behavior increases.

and efficient operations, but also more contented, creative, and productive people. In the future, the world will be led by the societies,
organizations, and individuals that value and ensure dignity for all.

"For his book Good to Great, *Jim Collins sifted through the
1,435 firms that have ever been in the Fortune 500. He found
only 11 firms that demonstrated periods of exceptional performance. Notably, all 11 had CEOs who were…humble. 'Hum-
ble' is Collins's word, and by it he means a CEO who would
listen to anyone, anytime, who might have something to offer
to the CEO's quest for success. In other words, these CEOs elim-
inated every trace of rankism from their work lives—and they,
and their companies, won big."*

—Robert Knisely in *Washington Monthly* (April 2003)

KEY POINTS

- It is possible to have rank without rankism.

- It is also possible to interrupt the cycle of rankism, in which
  rankism begets more rankism.

- Rank in itself is not the problem; rank can be useful, good, and
  necessary. Rankism—*the abuse of rank*—is the problem.

- When rank is used to protect the dignity of all, a culture of
  dignity is created.

- Dignitarian environments produce higher performing organizations than do environments with high levels of rankism.

chapter four

Rankism 101

We don't have to look very far to find examples of rankism in our own lives. We all recognize it, because we've all experienced it. Most likely, we have played both roles: target and perpetrator. That's the nature of rankism—and it's a key feature that distinguishes it from other "isms". We keep our basic skin color all our lives, but we aren't a nobody (perceived to be "unimportant" or of low rank) or a somebody (perceived to be "important" or of high rank) forever. Our rank is not fixed, as our membership in another group may be. We may be a somebody at work but a nobody at home, or vice versa. We may be treated as a somebody in middle age but as a nobody when we retire. Our rank shifts at different times and in different contexts. The result is that we are all somebodies some of the time, and nobodies at other times, but no one is a somebody all of the time!

Rankism is Everywhere

As you use the filter of rankism to look at the world, you may begin to

"It's comforting to know that a lot of the insults I've put up with in my life are being experienced by people everywhere. I, for one, am sick of being nobodied."

—From www.dignityforall.org

see rankism everywhere. That's normal. Once we have a word for something, we are able to notice things that were difficult to see without it.
The following anecdotes begin to give a sense of just how pervasive
rankism is: People experience rankism everywhere, everyday, at all
ages, and in all walks of life.

The Pervasiveness of Rankism: Examples from Daily Life

**From an English-
man living in the
United States:**

I had occasion to visit the Social Security Administration and could
hear that blacks at the head of the line were being treated disre-
spectfully. I was about to attribute this to American racism when I
realized that the civil servants behind the counters who were dishing
out the insults were themselves black. It doesn't make much sense
to call denigration of this sort "racism," but that's how it would be
described if the bureaucrats were white.

—Simon W.

**From a mother of young
children:**

I left the "working world" from the time my first child was born until
my second entered preschool. Except for nap times, stretches without
the children were rare. We couldn't afford babysitters on one salary.
Once in a while we'd manage to escape and attend parties given by
my husband's co-workers, most of them young and child-free. At first
I looked forward to getting out into the adult world again, but soon
I began to dread it because of the inevitable question, "And what do
you do?" Having never before worked so hard, on call 24 hours a day
and overwhelmed by the demands of two toddlers, I began to resent
being made to feel apologetic for being "just" a mom.

—Janet H.

From a federal official:

Going from eighth grade to freshman year in high school was traumatic for me. I was awkward, skinny, and had poor social skills. Almost from the beginning, I was teased by the other students, both boys and girls.

One of my most vivid memories is of getting so frustrated that I started to hit one of the jocks. The other guys had to pull him off, or he would have really creamed me. Shortly after that, I went trick-or-treating with these guys at Halloween and, taking a dare, I threw a lawn chair on someone's porch, just to be accepted.

One thing I did to make myself noticed was carry a $100 bill to school, show it to everyone, and then tear it in half.

I also had an act where people would point their finger at me like a gun, say "bang, bang," and I would moan and groan and fall over in a death agony. At least I was noticed. I'd even do it while driving, throwing my arms out the driver's side window and flopping down the outside of the car door for as long as I could before losing control of the vehicle.

—Thomas P.

From a political consultant:

At Washington cocktail parties people ask what you do for a living during the first 30 seconds of the conversation. When I was executive director of a national nonprofit working on transportation safety issues, I was of no interest to the would-be movers and shakers. They would simply walk away from me (sometimes without even a contrived exit line). But when I started working for a news organization, things changed. Because the media is considered to be a second god to government, a shadow power unto itself, these same people suddenly gave me their full attention. Similarly, when my wife became a producer for *All Things Considered* at National Public Radio, people started to give her attention in a way they never had before. Some of them even started "playing me" in the hopes that I would help them get to her.

—Anthony G.

From a book editor:

During my freshman year at college I enrolled in a course in English literature. There were only about 16 students and I was looking forward to the kind of learning experience that a small class would afford. The professor conducted the first meeting in his home. As a kind of "getting to know you exercise" he began with, "I'd like all of you to introduce yourselves and tell the rest of us what your father does for a living." I was dumbfounded. My father was a bus driver. He was a hard-working man and had always taken satisfaction in the fact that he could send me to this prestigious school without even a request for financial aid. Knowing that he was proud of himself and of me, and that suddenly I felt ashamed of him, made the shame doubly acute. One by one the students introduced themselves and followed with their glamorous pedigrees: "My father is a Dean of Harvard Medical School." "My father teaches at Temple." "My father is an attorney." As my turn approached I felt my mouth getting dry. I simply couldn't bear to tell the truth. I introduced myself and followed with a quick "My father is a transportation engineer."

—Jan K.

From a therapist's observations of sexual harassment:

The dean of the law school would hit on the lower paid workers, groping them, but would flirt only verbally with the high-ranked staff (e.g., the registrar). The liberties he took were a function of women's rank and position. The ones who didn't get paid much got fondled; the more highly paid got cozied up to but were spared any greater humiliation.

—Name withheld by request

From a woman in her late forties:

Upon graduating from college I took a job in food service at a local university teaching hospital to earn money for graduate studies in music. My job—delivering trays to patients while wearing a polyester uniform and hair net—was certainly not a glamorous one. Often, as I wielded my cumbersome cart through the halls, I was blocked by clusters of medical interns on their rounds. They exuded self-importance and ignored me and I was forced to maneuver ever so carefully around them. After a while, in anger and frustration, I would deliberately run over toes. One day I stepped into an elevator in which there were two handsome young male interns. One looked at me, smiled and gave me a shy, friendly "Hi." I returned the smile and hello. His buddy, eyeing the exchange, nudged him and said to him in a low snicker, "Slumming in the elevator?" That was 25 years ago and I still remember it. To this day I regret not having had the presence of mind to object to his behavior.

—Janet K.

From a woman reminiscing about herself as a seventh grader:

I was in the out-group. I was a sweet, sensitive girl who followed all the rules, but I was ugly. Frizzy hair. Big nose. Bad skin. Often I'd come home in tears because of the teasing from my classmates.

I remember there was a school talent show. Tim, a fellow outcast, somehow gathered the courage to sing "The House of the Rising Sun." He'd probably imagined this moment over and over—it was his chance to be somebody. Well, as soon as he got up on stage and started singing, the catcalls started. He could barely finish his song.

You'd think that after being the target of similar abuse I might have stood up for him, or at least stayed quiet. But instead, I joined in the jeering. "Yeah, that Tim is such a jerk." I felt so relieved that for once the target wasn't me.

—Claire S.

From a contractor recalling his days as an apprentice carpenter:

Most of the contractors I worked for during my apprenticeship were "screamers." If you asked for help, they'd yell, "You should know that by now." If you made a mistake it was the end of the world.

There are contractors who just put you on foundations. You never get a chance to do the framing or the trim work; you're just a grunt. How can you learn the trade like that? And when they're through with you they send you down the road.

The worst is working for a contractor who has his son working, or a cousin, nephew, or friend. As someone without connections, you get the digging, the form stripping, the concrete pouring. You're also expected to have a good attitude. Only the boss's relatives are allowed to bitch. You feel that you're judged on a whim and not on what you produce.

One contractor told me, "All I want to see are your elbows and your ass." He wanted me bent over, working at all times. Even lunch was a walking sandwich. The ultimate humiliation is when contractors don't provide temporary toilet facilities, so you have to relieve yourself in the bushes.

—Chris C.

From a top executive who, at 45, quit to try something new:

I had a succession of ever more impressive business cards during my career. On my way up the ladder, they defined me—title and company. The response was always very positive. When I retired I printed up new business cards with only my name, address, and phone number. The response to this name-only ID was that I had become a nobody. Without title and institutional affiliation, people didn't know how to calibrate my value. They no longer saw me as having anything to offer, and for several years, I'm sorry to say, I believed this myself.

—Peter C.

From a young woman with cerebral palsy who is training to be a therapist:

People are always telling me what to do. Older women will see me outside and say, "Where's your coat?" I know it's due to my disability. Respect doesn't come easily. I often feel dismissed when someone without a disability wouldn't be.

At work people think it's OK to belittle me in front of others. My boss calls me "sweetie" and "honey," but when I do something she doesn't like she's quick to criticize.

Often employers have acted as though they were doing me a favor by hiring me, and then used that as an excuse to pay me less. Once I get an advanced degree and have a private therapy practice, I think this kind of discrimination will disappear.

What really brought the importance of a higher degree home to me was a dissertation I read on physically disabled women whose children were taken away from them by state agencies. In every instance, the women who lost their children were poor and uneducated. I simply *have* to be in school. If I'm middle class with an academic job, then nobody will be able to take my children away.

—Jody S.

Types and Levels of Rankism

Rankism can manifest in many different ways, in different contexts. [*See Sidebars: Additional Ways Rankism May Manifest, and Institutional Rankism.*]

Additional Ways Rankism May Manifest

The word *rankism* can also refer to the use of power illegitimately obtained (such as when voting machines are tampered with, to ensure that one candidate receives the most votes).

Rankism can include a whole host of other behaviors as well, for example...

What somebodies do to nobodies (e.g., ignore, shun, silence, put down verbally, humiliate)

(continued)

When the personal interests of rank-holders (e.g., clergy, school teachers and administrators, CEOs, board members of organizations, elected representatives) are placed above those they serve (e.g., congregation members, students, staff or clients, shareholders, voting constituents)

When the interests of somebodies (the powerful in a given context) are given priority over the legitimate interests of nobodies (the less powerful in that context), e.g., administrators' interests over the legitimate interests of teachers' or students', or parents' interests over the legitimate interests of their children

Damaging assertion of rank (e.g., a mugging)

The presumption of superiority

Abusive, discriminatory, or exploitative behavior towards those with less power

Using the power of position to secure unwarranted advantages or benefits for oneself

Self-aggrandizement

Inflicting indignity on others

Rankism can and does occur at every level of human relationship, including:

- Interpersonal rankism (between and among individuals)
- Intra- and inter-group rankism (within and between groups)
- Organizational rankism (within or by organizations)
- Governmental rankism (within or by governing bodies)
- Societal rankism (within societies)
- Global rankism (in international relations)
- Institutionalized rankism (when rankism becomes institutionalized in a society, e.g., a permanent underclass of the working poor develops, for whom social mobility is a myth)

- Inter-species rankism (between species; i.e., humans' misuse of rank vis-à-vis other animals)

- Ecological rankism (using our power as humans to exploit the ecological environment of our planet)

Regardless of the context, type, or level of rankism, the underlying cause is always the same: *the belief that our perceived superiority over another person or group licenses us to misuse the power that our position or rank gives us.*

Institutionalized Rankism

When rankism becomes institutionalized, it has become so deeply embedded in a system that political, social, and organizational structures continually reinforce rankist attitudes and practices. As a result, it can be extremely difficult for individuals to break free of the limitations imposed by the rankism that is built into the system. Barbara Ehrenreich, in her book *Nickel and Dimed: On (Not) Getting By in America* (New York: Owl Books, 2002), vividly describes how rankism marginalizes the working poor, keeping them in their place while their low salaries effectively make goods and services available to society at subsidized prices, i.e., rankism has made the working poor the unacknowledged and obligatory philanthropists of American society.

Microinequities

Rankist actions can be so small that people hardly notice them; yet their cumulative effect can be devastating, to both the individuals who experience them and the organizations in which they occur. The pervasiveness of such commonplace slights, known as microinequities, have led major companies to provide training for employees in how and why to stop them. [*See Sidebar, Microinequities: Little Things Matter.*]

Microinequities: Little Things Matter

The following is abridged and adapted from "Diversity Training and Microinequities: Ensuring All Voices Are Valued," by Emily Hollis, *Chief Learning Officer* magazine, May 19, 2004.

You're repeatedly interrupted by your boss. When you offer an idea in a meeting it's ignored; but your colleague says the same thing two minutes later and the idea is praised, and then adopted. Your name is left off the staff e-mail announcement list. You sit in your supervisor's office while she interrupts her conversation with you to take a call on her cell phone.

These are microinequities, "the small, subtle behaviors that devalue other people," says Brigid Moynahan, founder of the Next Level, a leadership training firm. And the business world has begun to worry about them. Though they are small and subtle, the impact of microinequities can be large, so large that companies like Chubb, JPMorgan, and Johnson & Johnson have made microinequities training a central part of their diversity initiatives. They teach management how not to drive employees away through repeated subtle actions that communicate a lack of value.

For those who experience them, the cumulative effect of microinequities can result in loss of confidence, motivation, creativity, and difficulty maintaining a positive attitude. Sometimes, people may not even know what's bothering them. Says Moynahan, "We don't know that what's happening are subtle discounts that are building up inside and making us feel like we don't have value."

Microinequities are a form of rankism, subtle to detect, but powerful in their effects.

The following contemplation exercise is intended to guide you to new insights about your own experiences of rankism and dignity. We've found it helpful to have one person read it slowly to one or more people, when possible, to maximize the effect. [*See Sidebar, Guided Contemplation: Memories of Rankism, Memories of Dignity.*]

GUIDED CONTEMPLATION

Memories of Rankism

First, start by taking a few moments to relax. See if you can adopt an attitude of curiosity.

Now, ask yourself, "When have I been treated in a rankist way?" (Wait for something to come to mind.)

What feelings did the experience of rankism evoke in you at the time? What feelings are present now? Just notice the feelings, knowing that they are a natural response to rankism. As you hold them in your awareness, allow them to dissolve.

Next, ask yourself, "When have I treated others in a rankist way? What feelings did your attitudes or actions produce in you? What might the other person or people have felt? What are your feelings now? Again, notice and allow the feelings.

Memories of Dignity

Next, ask yourself, "When have I been treated with dignity?"

What feelings did the experience of dignity evoke in you? What feelings are present now? Notice those feelings.

And now, ask yourself "When have I treated others with dignity?"

What feelings did your actions evoke in you? What feelings do you imagine were evoked in the other person?

Allow yourself to experience the effects of dignity.

KEY POINTS:

- Our rank shifts, depending on the context. That means we may be either a somebody or a nobody, depending on the context and the time; and we have all probably been both a target and a perpetrator of rankism.

- Rankism is pervasive. Once you know about rankism, you start to see it everywhere.

chapter five

Groundbreakers and Trailblazers: That's You!

Because abuse of rank is so commonplace, people are often unaware that their behavior is rankist; even people who are targets of it may not recognize it as rankism. Most of us are so used to people routinely abusing their rank that we consider it "normal" behavior.

It can therefore be helpful to recognize that those who speak up or take action to address rankism are trailblazers at the leading edge of change. If you are reading this book, you are probably a trailblazer, too; and so you may run into obstacles when you try to un-do rankism in different areas of your life. You may find that some people are not receptive to the ideas expressed here. They may dismiss the entire idea of rankism, try to sidetrack the discussion into a debate about rank, or get defensive when you speak up or take action. They may even retaliate. *All of that is normal at the beginning of any change in human consciousness.*

When Galileo asserted that the earth revolves around the sun and not vice versa, he was put under house arrest. For a long time afterward, those who accepted the idea were subject to various forms of rankism, including silencing or simple ridicule. In South Africa, as the movement to end apartheid began, it was extremely dangerous to speak out against it. During the American civil rights movement, people risked their lives if they advocated against racism. Many sacrificed their freedom and their lives so that future generations could live in a world free of discrimination or oppression based on skin color.

You take risks, even in the current era, whenever you speak with an awareness that goes beyond the current collective understanding. You may make sacrifices so that future generations will be able to live in a world free of discrimination or oppression based on rank.

We say this both as a cautionary note and so you won't become discouraged as you take steps to end rankism. It may take time, but a collective shift of understanding about dignity and rankism *will* take place eventually, because rankism is not an adaptive behavior for a species that has the technological capacity to destroy itself. (For example, everyday rankism by managers in organizations can silence voices that would otherwise help avoid major technological disasters. *[See Sidebar, Rankism in Organizations: Lessons from NASA, p. 43.]* And misusing one's power over others, from personal interactions to global relations, tends to lead to retaliation, easily escalating rankist behavior to potentially dangerous levels.) As we humans, as a species, begin to understand the harmful consequences of allowing rankism in our world, we will learn to disallow it—and will teach our children to do the same.

KEY POINTS:

- Creating a dignitarian society is pioneering work; those who speak up for dignity are trailblazers.

- It is normal for trailblazers to run into obstacles.

- It may take time, but the world will become more dignitarian eventually, because rankism is not an adaptive behavior for a species that has the technological capacity to destroy itself.

chapter six

Talking About Rankism

One of the best ways to end rankism is to simply start talking about it. Until now, the subject of rankism has been taboo, not discussable in polite company. It's not always comfortable to say "You know, we might be excluding others here, depriving them of an opportunity to be heard. Let's see if we can listen to some other voices, too." Or, "Hey guys, do you think we're giving enough people a chance at this job? How about letting more people in on the action?"

People don't typically enjoy confronting their own rankism. Those in positions of power may not want to "rock the boat" with their friends or colleagues, and when those of lower rank speak up, they may risk retaliation. The unfortunate truth is that although we may not mind indulging in rankism, when our rankism is exposed, we mind. So we just don't talk about it.

The Discomfort of Exposure

Most of us, deep down, recognize that insulting another's dignity is morally objectionable. So when we are found to be engaging in the behavior, we feel uncomfortable. We may feel embarrassed, guilty, or ashamed. We may respond in anger toward the person or circumstance that exposed our rankism, even as we justify our actions.

The Risk of Invisibility

As already noted, rankism occurs so commonly that most people just accept it as unavoidable and inevitable. This, however, is a dangerous stance for a species to take (though it may sometimes be a useful survival mechanism for an individual). It is dangerous because when we accept rankism as the natural state of affairs, the rankism that is everywhere becomes *transparent*, and hence invisible to us. We see *through* it, but we can't *see* it. Like the air we breathe, rankism permeates our environments. We don't see the rankism that is all around us because we're immersed in it, and because we tend to have a blind spot regarding our own rankism.

Making Rankism Discussable

If we want to end rankism, we first have to see it, and we can often see it best by talking about it. Discussing rankism allows it to come into view. By naming and describing it, we are able to actually *see* it, rather than see *through* it. Discussing the undiscussable makes the unseeable seen.

Lifting the Taboo

When rankism becomes discussable, not only does it begin to be seen, it also begins to be seen as *unacceptable*. And then it becomes easier for people to speak up about it. It becomes easier, for example, for a member of a clique or power group to say, "Hey, isn't that rankism? Let's find a way to listen to some other points of view before we decide." Or, "Since we have committed to creating a dignitarian workplace, could we see if there is another way to approach this?"

Two ways to begin breaking the taboo are to 1) Start a dialogue about how you or your organization can be more dignitarian [*See Sidebar, Starting Dialogue*], and 2) Point out rankism when it occurs [*See Sidebar, Don't Let Rankism Go By*].

Starting Dialogue

One way to begin breaking the taboo about discussing rankism is to have an open-ended dialogue with others about how you can be more inclusive. Brigid Moynahan, a consultant to Fortune 500 companies, suggests that executives and managers have a dialogue with their work teams about behaviors that exclude people. The idea is to build teamwork and eliminate microinequities, which are a form of rankism. [*See Sidebar, Chapter 4.*] She offers the following questions to get the conversation started. They are appropriate for other settings as well where people want to raise awareness about rankism and begin conversations about dignity.

- Do you feel…included…respected…valued?
- What behaviors wall people out?
- What behaviors encourage contribution?
- What can we start, stop, do more of?
- What can I do differently?
- What can the team do differently?
- What can senior management do differently?

—Questions are from "Go Ahead: Sweat the Small Stuff" by Brigid Monahan,
Executive Action, The Conference Board, No. 151, June 2005

Don't Let Rankism Go By

Candace Blase tells of standing in a crowd waiting for luggage at a carousel in the Sacramento airport. Nearby, two women were unself-consciously and loudly voicing their prejudices against lesbians. Candace turned to them and said, "I couldn't help but overhear your conversation. I'm a lesbian, and I don't think I'm that bad or dangerous."

By speaking evenly, without anger or accusation, Candace made it possible for the women to take in and consider her words instead of defensively lashing back.

Speaking Effectively

To be effective when speaking about or confronting rankism, there are a few principles we like to keep in mind. [*For additional suggestions, see Sidebar, Speaking Up Effectively, Chapter 7.*]

Dignity

Keep everyone's dignity intact is the cardinal rule of a dignitarian society. Since dignity is our birthright, it needs to be honored at all times, in all circumstances, with all people—even, and especially, with those who are not honoring our dignity. Although our reflex reactions are often to respond to indignity with further indignity, it is only by modeling dignity ourselves that others will learn how to do it. And it is by practicing dignity in challenging situations that we hone our own dignitarian skills.

Truth

In general, if something is important enough to address, it should be addressed accurately and directly—either by taking your concern to the person you're upset with, or by talking about it to someone who can help you formulate a strategy for addressing the problem. Telling the truth is, of course, basic to establishing trust in any relationship; not being truthful to or about someone can be a way of insulting their dignity.

If leaders are wise, they will provide opportunities for people to discuss their complaints and concerns openly—through an ombudsperson, for example, or via regularly scheduled conversations with the leadership. Otherwise, rank holders invite under-the-radar conversations, as people express their dissatisfaction to others, try to make sense of overt or covert behavior in the organization, or vent their frustrations about rankism over which they seem to have no control.

Tact

Telling the truth doesn't mean being rude or unkind—or rankist! It means speaking the truth as you perceive it as accurately, kindly, and gently as possible (and it may not always be possible). Tact is a skill that can be learned through practice.

Tactics

The climate of rankism in the world today resembles the climate of racism for blacks in the United States in the 1930s and '40s. Racism then was everywhere, as rankism today is everywhere; many, if not most, people encounter rankism all the time, all day long. In the 1930s and '40s, if blacks had spoken up every time they experienced racism, they wouldn't have had many silent moments, and many would not have survived. In that era, there could be very serious consequences, including death, for anyone attempting to combat racism.

Extreme consequences for exposing rankism may seem rarer now, but they exist, notably in totalitarian regimes. Even when consequences are not as extreme, most efforts to counteract rankism at this time do carry with them some risk. You may, for example, risk losing your job, your status with high-ranking people, being shunned by friends or colleagues, humiliation, or being subjected to further indignities. So, be tactical. Sometimes you may choose not to speak up if it isn't a battle you feel prepared or compelled to take on.

Patience

Progress usually takes time. If you can be patient with progress when it doesn't happen overnight, and you can be patient with yourself when you seem to make mistakes, you'll be less stressed. Remember, too, that you can't always see the effects of your actions. Your efforts may not always appear to produce positive results, but that may be because we are still in the early stages of change. Each time you speak up, you send a message, which makes it easier for the next person who dares to break the taboo. As people repeatedly encounter the message of dignity for all, it begins to sink in.

KEY POINTS:

- Talking about rankism is taboo, but we need to talk about it in order to be able to stop it.

- When we talk about rankism, it begins to be seen as unacceptable, and then it becomes easier to counteract.

- Two ways to begin breaking the taboo against discussing rankism are to 1) Start a dialogue about how you or your organization can be more dignitarian, and 2) Point out rankism when it occurs.

- To speak effectively about rankism, it can help to keep these principles in mind: Keep Everyone's Dignity Intact, Be Truthful, Be Tactful, Be Tactical, and Have Patience.

chapter seven

Identifying and Targeting Rankism

"Rankism is far more encompassing than racism, sexism, or ageism. Rankism must be our prime target from now on."

—Studs Terkel, Pulitzer Prize-winning author of *Working* and *The Good War*

O nce we can talk about rankism, we can start to target it specifically, stopping it wherever we find it. To do that, we need to first identify rankism in our own attitudes and behaviors, as well as in others'.

Identifying Rankism in Ourselves and Others

Rankism can be harder to identify in yourself than in other people, but it is also easier to correct. Hard as it may be to change yourself, it is usually easier to change your own attitudes and behaviors than it is to persuade, convince, or force others to change theirs. For this reason, it can be helpful to address your own and others' rankism simultaneously. Here is a simple method we find useful:

　1.　Notice rankist attitudes and behaviors in other people. Some possible questions to ask:

   a. Did someone try to make you feel like a nobody?

   b. Did a person or group silence people's expression of legitimate concerns?

   c. Were you or someone else threatened or humiliated?

2. Look at where you may be exhibiting similar tendencies or behaviors (even if yours seem less obvious).

3. Work to change your own rankist attitudes and behaviors, even as you stand up for your own dignity and help to establish new standards of dignity for all.

"How easily we put down those we see as subordinate in title or wealth or origin; how silently we cringe at another's assumption of superiority. I saw myself in some of the examples, and I shuddered."

—Anthony Lewis, Pulitzer Prize-winning former columnist for *The New York Times*, commenting on examples of rankism in the book *Somebodies and Nobodies: Overcoming the Abuse of Rank*

A Key Indicator: An Attitude of Superiority

Sometimes rankism is not a visible behavior. It can show up as an attitude of superiority or a closed mind. For example, a mind that closes itself off to outside influence may think—consciously or unconsciously, voluntarily or involuntarily—"I'm right and you're wrong, and therefore I'm better." "I know. You don't—and so I'm superior."

This kind of rankist thinking may be found in any domain, e.g., ideological, religious, or academic. It is generally present when people believe their view to be the one right way. It flourishes wherever people pride themselves on knowing the truth or being more knowledgeable or capable than others. We may not be able to completely eliminate rankist thinking, but we can certainly learn to identify it and to stop any rankist behaviors that may issue from such thoughts.

Overt Rankism

Overt rankism would include behavior such as firing a whistle-blower—
someone who exposed an organizational practice that higher-ranking
people within the organization did not want exposed. This phenomenon
is well recognized in business and government settings, but is also present
elsewhere, such as in non-profit organizations and religious institutions.
These often have fewer built-in protections for workers, e.g., no unions or
fair treatment policies, or they may have governance structures that foster
rankism because there are few checks and balances to safeguard dignity.

For example, in some organizations it is standard practice to hold
so-called "elections" for seats on the governing body, but in fact,
members are not allowed any choice when voting. Instead, members'
only option is to ratify a single slate of "nominees." This enables new
representatives to be hand-picked either by a single person in charge
or a few people appointed by the governing body to make the nomina-
tions. This kind of system facilitates rank abuse. Interested and capable
people may be deliberately or inadvertently excluded. The observable
result is a silencing or under-representation of voices that are not part
of the dominant power group.

Groups may sometimes legitimately choose to operate with non-
democratic processes, such as appointment of individuals to a governing
board, rather than elections. In such cases, it is important to consider the
kinds of safeguards that may help ensure that rankism does not infect the
process, such as announcing in advance any openings to be filled and
soliciting from the entire membership names of interested individuals.

Covert Rankism

Covert or hidden rankism might include giving a bogus reason for
terminating the employment of a whistleblower (e.g., "We're restruc-
turing the department."); or, not promoting an employee whose work
performance is excellent but cultural background is different from the
supervisor's.

Hidden rankism is more subtle than blatantly rankist behavior, and
therefore can be more challenging to address. Moreover, these subtle

forms of rankism are often part of accepted organizational practices, so they tend to be invisible to most people. Exposing these forms of rankism requires articulating "what's wrong" with the behavior—as well as what is preferable about dignitarian behavior—to people who do not yet have a conceptual framework for understanding these issues.

In such cases, methods must be found to educate one or more people in the organization about rankism and its relation to dignity. For example, a general article about rankism and dignity could be published in the organization's newsletter. You may also try to enlist the aid of high-rank holders, explaining to them the principles behind your efforts. If recruitment of high-ranking individuals is not an option, or fails when tried, the next step may be to band together with others to effect change as a group.

Effects of Rankism

Sometimes rankism is most easily identified by observing the effects it has on individuals or a group. These might be physiological, emotional, psychological, mental, spiritual, behavioral, or organizational. When we notice certain feelings or conditions, we can look to see if they may be traceable to experiences of rank abuse, and then take action to target the rankism that produced the effect.

Effects on Individuals

Negative emotions

Effects of rankism on individuals may include such feelings as shame, humiliation, anxiety, fear, anger, rage, low self-esteem, insecurity, depression, paralysis, loss of confidence, and/or reduced ability to focus or process information.

Stress

Being subjected to indignity produces stress and can trigger potentially debilitating emotional or physical responses. Stress reactions typical to a given individual, such as rapid breathing, sweaty palms, difficulty sleeping, confusion, or nervousness, are symptoms that may have rankism as their source.

Speaking Up Effectively

Here are a few ideas for speaking up effectively to target rankism.

- Aim to educate. Give a person or group who is displaying rankist behavior the summary of rankism and its consequences and remedies available at www.dignityforall.org.

- Approach the other person or group as an ally, from the viewpoint that you are all on the same team and all want to create a climate of dignity.

- Use "I" statements, as much as possible, rather than "you" statements that appear to blame. For example, saying, "When you did that, I felt angry, hurt, and humiliated. I felt as if my dignity had been assaulted. Could we talk about some other ways the issue might have been addressed?" This models a way to speak about the impact the other person's rankism has had on you and provides a basis for an exploratory conversation in which both parties are free to truthfully share their experiences and explore other options for behavior.

- Take an inquiring stance, seeking to understand the other person's possible motivations and framework for thinking.

- Gently—and, as much as possible, without judgment—explain that the behavior the other has engaged in is rankist and why. Try to offer an alternative way that the person or group could have addressed the issue.

Effects on Organizations

Reduced productivity and revenue

Loss of productivity and reduced revenue are measurable by-products of a culture of rankism in organizations, largely because people need to expend so much effort to defend themselves against assaults on their dignity. Mental attention is simply not available for focused and productive work. Creativity, ability to solve problems and respond to crises, and capacity to learn are impaired.

Crisis management

Relatively small problems can turn into major crises because of rankist behavior. Silencing of "whistleblowers," truth tellers, or dissenters, for example, can mean loss of information crucial to organizational functioning. This, in turn, reduces the organization's capacity to effect optimal outcomes. Before the 1986 U.S. space shuttle disaster, lower ranking individuals within NASA repeatedly tried to call attention to the shuttle's faulty O-rings, later found to be the source of the shuttle explosion. Higher-ranking officials silenced those voices, the launch occurred as planned, and the shuttle blew up minutes later. [*See Sidebar, Rankism in Organizations: Lessons from NASA.*]

Widespread system dysfunction

Employees and other members of an organization are affected emotionally by rankism and this can result in widespread system dysfunction. Loss of loyalty, acts of revenge or sabotage, and passing on rankist behavior to others lower in rank are some of the behaviors that can result from rankism in an organization. From a systems perspective, rankism produces dispersed, generalized anxiety in the overall system. A system with anxiety in it will act out that anxiety through individuals—who may be labeled as "troublemakers," "dysfunctional individuals," or other names. Individuals thus get blamed for the problems of the system, when in fact they are primarily acting out the dysfunction of the system, the root cause of which is rankism.

Effects on Societies

System malfunctions, such as public health problems and national disasters

At the societal level, rankism produces effects similar to those at individual and organizational levels, but on a broader scale. Within nations, for example, infringements of the people's dignity occur when legal standards of safety in hazardous industries are set

Rankism in Organizations: Lessons from NASA

The *Mars Climate Orbiter* mission failure in 1979 was due in part to what might be called technological rankism. It starts with an unquestioning reverence for those who are anointed as experts or who assume that mantle on their own. All too often, they stifle discussion and quash dissension on technical issues—a form of technical intimidation.

During the flight to Mars there were early warning signs that something was wrong in the trajectory analysis, but the navigation team wouldn't listen. When problems were pointed out they essentially said, "Trust us. We're the experts." Due to a software error, the spacecraft entered too low in the Martian atmosphere and consequently burnt up. This was foreseeable during the flight and could have been corrected, but we caved in to the insistence of the navigation team that everything would be all right. That's technological rankism.

A similar dynamic is well documented in the shuttle disasters. Prior to the *Challenger* flight, engineers had warned that the unusually low temperature [in Florida the night before the launch] could be a problem for the O-rings. In this case, pressure by management to launch on time silenced engineering concerns. This wasn't technological rankism; rather, it was garden-variety managerial rankism that led to one of our most vivid national disasters.

The *Columbia* accident investigation report shows a similar phenomenon: As what the board calls an 'informal chain of command' began to shape [the flight's] outcome, location in the structure empowered some to speak and silenced others."

Rankism was a major contributing cause of both shuttle disasters.

—Dr. Noel Hinners, former director of NASA's Goddard Space Flight Center
and former director of the Smithsonian National Air and Space Museum

lower than is healthful for the population or when illegal safety violations are not prosecuted. Permitting businesses to maintain practices known to cause public health problems—such as injury or death among coal miners, or illnesses like asthma, mercury poisoning, or types of cancers associated with environmental pollutants—is rankist, and these forms of rankism can have powerful and damaging effects.

International tensions

On a national and international scale, rankism can result in the inability to resolve issues that naturally arise from differences among peoples; in bullying of smaller, less powerful countries by larger nations; and in terrorism, which is both a form of rankism toward others and a method for retaliation and revenge.

Complex social ills

Rankism is a contributing factor to a wide range of societal problems, such as illiteracy and crime. The complex relationships that exist between rankism and various social ills merits study and consideration as we move toward a more dignitarian world.

KEY POINTS:

- **To effectively target rankism, we first need to identify it, in ourselves and others.**

- **Rankism is both attitudinal and behavioral, and it can be overt or covert.**

- **Sometimes rankism can best be identified by observing its detrimental effects—on individuals, organizations, and societies. Then we can identify and target the rankist treatment that produced the effects.**

chapter eight

Detecting Warning Signs of Rankism

S ome rankist behaviors are so prevalent that they deserve special mention as signs to watch out for when building a culture of dignity. The following practices and behaviors are often used— knowingly or unknowingly—to put or keep others down.

Secrecy and Silencing

Both secrecy and silencing are commonly used by people in power to maintain the rights and privileges associated with their rank. Dictators and despots, prime ministers and presidents, lay and clerical religious leaders, school administrators, CEOs and mid-level managers—all these and many others may use secrecy about their own activities and silencing of dissenting voices to maintain power or control. They may or may not be conscious of doing it.

Secrecy keeps rankism invisible

When leaders make decisions in secret, take actions in secret, or hide the truth about events that should not be secret, others are unable to examine the leaders' actions to determine whether they are fair and just and honor everyone's dignity. The Federal Open

Meetings Laws offer one kind of safeguard against the rankism that secrecy breeds. The statutes specify the conditions under which certain agencies and committees of the government, including a public school district's governing body, may meet to discuss business. The laws include a requirement that business be transacted only at meetings which members of the public and press are permitted to attend. It also includes regulations about the percentage of members required to be in attendance for discussion of board business. If more organizations were to follow the Open Meetings model, there would be fewer opportunities for them to fall into the patterns of secrecy that foster rankism.

Silencing creates an environment in which rankism thrives
Silencing is a companion to secrecy. By silencing or ignoring voices that may raise questions, call attention to potential problems, express disagreement with the actions of those in decision-making positions, or offer creative solutions to vexing problems, rank holders "keep the people in their place," maintain their own authority and control, and insult the dignity of others.

The human need to be heard is violated when avenues are not created through which all involved may express their voices and be genuinely listened to.

Many leaders fail to understand that secrecy and silencing are never healthy practices for an organization. They create an environment in which rankism thrives, and the consequences are organizational dysfunction. Often, people who have dared to raise their voices or expose rankist practices are blamed for the organization's problems, when in fact the source of dysfunction is the system's tolerance of practices that support rankism.

Snobbery

Snobbery is a form of elitism
Snobbery is making oneself out to be "better than" others, and treating them accordingly. Snobbery, of course, is rampant at all levels of

society. Children learn it early in life. They learn, for example, to treat classmates who live in "less desirable" areas of town or who don't wear the latest fashions as if they are inferior.

Snobbish behavior is often displayed by cliques. Most people know the indignity of being ignored, snubbed, insulted, banished, or barred from inclusion because they weren't part of "the right group" or power elite; or did not have the right occupation, education, point of view, financial status, clothes, or family history. Snobbery treats individuals and groups of people as if they are not as worthy, valued, or valuable because they lack certain characteristics which a self-identified "elite" group has deemed important.

The psychological toll snobbery takes is huge

Rankist attitudes are often internalized by those who are treated with this kind of disdain, resulting in low self-esteem and feelings of self-worth. Hurt, anger, sadness, grief, or the wish to "get even" are some of the emotional responses snobbery may evoke. This form of rankism often begets further rankism, as victims of the snobbery make internal vows not to remain at the bottom of the heap, learning instead to climb higher in the hierarchy—doing unto others as they have been done unto.

Bullying and Intimidation

Bullies use bravado, intimidation, and sheer force to maintain control and get their own way. The bully may be a kid on a playground calling another child names, a boss making clear to his staff that they are not free to express their views, or a superpower pressuring a smaller nation to support its U.N. resolution if it wants humanitarian aid. Bullying is a form of rankism and needs to be recognized as such, whether it is at home, on the playground, at the office, at worship, on reality TV, or on the big screen of global politics.

When bullying occurs, it is appropriate for others to help the one being bullied. Children, for example, need to be able to count on adults to stop bullies in their tracks and to help mediate disputes when necessary. It is also appropriate for higher-ranking individuals, organizations, or nations to use their rank to stop the bullying that occurs in the adult world. However, good judgment and care also need to be exercised. Sometimes our efforts to help can backfire and end up doing more harm than good (for example, in global relations).

Blackballing and Blacklisting

Blackballing and blacklisting (sometimes referred to as "white-listing" in communities of color) refer to the act of excluding someone from participating in a group, organization, or activity, usually on the basis of rank. Typically, blackballing and black- or white-listing are rankist behaviors because they illegitimately maintain the rank of those in power, perpetuating the elitism of the group. They exclude potential questioners, ensuring that any rankist behaviors will remain unchallenged.

Blackballing may not be overt. For example, people may be placed on a "mental blacklist"—not an actual, physical list—when they express opinions counter to those held by the people in higher ranking positions. Because leaders may be uncomfortable with disagreement, individuals who have expressed differing views may not be invited to participate in important meetings, sit on certain committees, or otherwise participate in the key workings of the organization. This kind of exclusion can be subtle and may not always be intentional. Sometimes rank-holders are simply avoiding the discomfort of having to deal with multiple perspectives. However, whether rankism is intentional or not, it is still rankism.

Backslapping and Its Derivatives: Backscratching, Old Boys' (or Girls') Networks, Nepotism, Friends Helping Friends

Friends and business associates exchange favors, tips about job openings or investment opportunities, special purchase deals—what's wrong with that? It's good to help others, isn't it?

Yes, it is. However, the behavior becomes rankist when it is exclusionary; and unfortunately, it is often more exclusionary than people realize.

People of similar rank and social or economic status tend to associate with each other. Hence, it is often not easy for others to "break in" to elite circles. Those who are not in the core group cannot gain access. The privileges and perks of rank, including the power that comes with it—which rank holders often take for granted—are denied to those who may not have had the same opportunities to acquire it.

Federally mandated Equal Employment hiring practices, affirmative action plans, and other strategies to open up exclusionary networks are intended to give individuals and groups of lower rank a more even chance to acquire the rights, privileges, and responsibilities of rank.

KEY POINTS:

- Secrecy and silencing are common forms of rankism. They create unhealthy environments that breed further rankism.

- Snobbery is a form of elitism that produces damaging psychological and emotional effects.

- Bullying and intimidation are also forms of rankism and therefore must be disallowed, whether on the school playground or in the international community of nations.

- Blackballing and black- or white-listing are rankist because they illegitimately maintain the rank of those in power, perpetuating elitism.

- "Backslapping" and its derivatives are rankist when they are exclusionary. "Friends helping friends" often becomes inadvertently rankist.

- Whether rankism is intentional or not, it is still rankism.

chapter nine

Standing Up to Rankism

O nce you have identified a rankist attitude or behavior, you will need to assess your options for responding. Could you, for example, talk to the people involved, discuss the matter with a higher-ranking individual, or write a letter to a local newspaper? The following approaches may help you select from the many available choices. [*A list of suggested resources is available at www.dignityforall.org.*]

Interpersonal

Approaches used in other disciplines, such as Marshall Rosenberg's non-violent communication training or physicist David Bohm's pioneering work on Deep Dialogue, can provide ideas, skills, and strategies for responding effectively to rankism, using an interpersonal approach. The "shalom building" process taught by psychologist and Protestant minister John Beck is usable in faith communities seeking to create a dignitarian environment, and can be adapted for secular contexts; diversity training can increase understanding and respect for others while helping individuals to develop communication and interpersonal skills; programs that raise awareness about microinequities and teach strategies for responding to cumulative

An Interpersonal Approach to Bullying

When ten-year-old Thomas Miller encountered bullying at school, he successfully confronted the situation using an interpersonal approach:

First, I went to the principal and told her about the bullying, but she didn't do anything about it. Then I talked to my dad, who made some suggestions. So I followed his advice and tried preventing it by helping my friends when they were being bullied. (Like when one boy took another boy's cap and started tossing it back and forth to other kids, to keep it away from the boy who owned it, I tried to catch it and give it back.) But then I—and a whole bunch of other kids —got in trouble and ended up in the principal's office.

Then one day my dad talked to one of the kids who was bullying, and it got better, because the boy's grandma was there and she told his mom. The boy felt bad for what he had done. Now there isn't any more bullying.

Doing what I did was hard. I had to have strength and courage.

slights to dignity can provide practical guidance about confronting rankism. Any process that emphasizes respect and dignity for all, while offering communication tools that foster careful listening and understanding, may be useful when approaching people you feel have violated your or others' dignity.

Organizational

An organizational response to rankism might focus on implementing governance processes that provide safeguards against rank abuse. Useful models for this already exist, such as the Carver governance model for non-profit boards, which provides a framework for establishing both strong governing boards and strong executive leadership. Other approaches emphasize strategies to ensure that all stakeholders have a voice in decision-making processes. [*See Resource D, How to Create a Culture of Dignity.*] From yet another angle, one labor union is considering introducing into collective bargaining negotiations an agreement to ensure a rankism-free workplace. All are ways of building a culture of dignity within an entire organization.

Feeling Like an Outsider? Take Action

To ensure people value and include you, it is important to get comfortable with a range of assertion strategies. When someone interrupts you, set a limit by telling the person you are not finished speaking. Left off a distribution list? Instead of allowing the action to erode your self-esteem, go to the person sending the message and ask to be included next time. Don't overreact. It is best to allow the person to "save face" by assuming the microinequity was unintentional. A small act of exclusion might not warrant a long and deep discussion. Often, it is simply enough to ask for a change in behavior. If the behavior was unintentional, the person will probably stop. On the other hand, if the person continues excluding you, more serious intervention may be required. You may want to take the person aside to iron out the issues in your professional relationship. If this doesn't work, you may need to seek outside help from a supervisor or Human Resources manager.

—From "Go Ahead: Sweat the Small Stuff" by Brigid Monahan,
Executive Action, The Conference Board, No. 151, June 2005

Political

If you are oriented toward political and social action, you might choose to organize your peers and colleagues, enlist allies of higher rank, join forces with other targets of rankism, and/or protest indignities as an organized group. [*See Sidebar, Political Organizing: Counteracting Rankism through Collective Action.*] One way to begin is by convening a small group of people to share experiences, raise awareness, learn together, and plan activities to help end rankism. [*See Sidebar, Banding Together: Affinity Groups to Address Rankism.*] Learning about others' efforts to bring about social and political change can help you create strategies and avoid possible pitfalls.

Psychological/Transformational

When targeting rankism, it is essential to attend to your own psychological well-being. The state of your own mind and emotions will have strong impact on your interactions. Maintaining clarity, good judgment, respect for others, and kindness and compassion, to the extent possible, is critical. Also helpful is the ability to forgive. [*See Chapter 10, Recovering from Rankism.*]

Many tools are available to help live through, learn from, and even grow as a result of rankism. They may involve approaches such as centering techniques, methods for clearing negative emotions, or ways of entering into non-judgmental and non-resistant states of awareness (in accordance with the old adage "What you resist persists"). The greater the psychological health and balance we ourselves can maintain, the more effective we will be in creating a dignitarian society for all.

Political Organizing: Counteracting Rankism through Collective Action

At several points in my life, I saw my mother mold a group of relatively weak people into a force powerful enough to confront and overturn rulings handed down autocratically by bureaucrats. In the 1950s, the Port of New York Authority, which is commonly perceived to be all-powerful in New York and New Jersey, decided that another international airport was needed to serve New York City. The site it chose was known as "The Great Swamp," an area of about 25 square miles. One part came within two miles of our home and a mile of the school attended by my brothers and me. The Great Swamp had blueberries growing in it. You could pick a ten-quart pail of them in an hour. Deer and other wildlife roamed about.

My mother organized a march on the capitol in Trenton, bursting into the chamber where the governor was giving a speech, with a banner that read, "Save our Swamp!" More importantly, the group found out who owned the swamplands and quietly bought up the property and made a gift of the land to the federal government for a wildlife preserve.

No airport was built. The townsfolk defeated the mighty Port Authority. Instead, Newark Airport was enlarged and today blueberries still grow and deer still live in New Jersey's Great Swamp.

In her later years, my mother organized the residents of retirement communities in Florida to lobby the state legislature on behalf of seniors, and founded a group called the "VIPs" to defend the rights of Visually Impaired Persons.

— Robert W. Fuller

Banding Together: Affinity Groups to Address Rankism

Where I work, employees can organize "affinity groups" for those with similar interests or experiences. I have recently started one that addresses rankism.

The rankism I am experiencing is mostly subtle. People expect me to know their name but don't know mine. Much of the dismissiveness is nonverbal: sighing impatiently; rolling eyeballs; taking things from my desk; using language that creates separateness from the work group, e.g., "We like you in your place at the front desk." When I did not recall the specifics of an employee's compensation package, a senior staff member said, "You are uninformed and should go back to the hills where you came from."

At first I wanted to resign, but did not have another job to transfer to. Now I find purpose in starting a group to address rankism. Some ideas I have for workshops are:

- Courageous communication: How to formulate an affirmative response that honors dignity when a rankist remark is made.

- Practicing verbal and non-verbal communication skills with the help of Theater of the Oppressed acting troupe.

I would think that rankist workplaces cost insurance companies more money—because rankism adversely affects health—and wonder if a survey instrument could be developed that would enable insurance companies to determine whether or not a company is rankist.

—Lisa L.

Spiritual

For the spiritually inclined, spiritual approaches to preserving and maintaining dignity can serve as powerful aids to personal and collective transformation. The civil rights movement drew significantly on the religious foundations of many of its early activists, including Mahatma Gandhi and Martin Luther King, Jr. Psychologist Robert Coles's work investigating the spirituality of children found that prayer helped children caught in the throes of the civil rights movement to maintain dignity and harmony as they encountered dangerous circumstances. Various religious and spiritual approaches offer their own methods and insights for responding to rankism.

Intuitive

A different approach to stopping rankism is to adopt an intuitive stance. When using this approach, logic and step-by-step planning may not always apply. The intuitive approach involves taking the stance that there is a deeper wisdom present and available to each of us. This "inner knowing" has instant access to "the whole picture," and, when followed, may provide solutions that circumvent linear processes. Following intuitive promptings has been known to trigger sudden shifts of awareness or attention, in either perpe-

Success Factors: Thoughtful Planning and Respectful Action

In the examples below, two groups of college students successfully curtailed rankist behavior on the part of their professors. In both cases, thoughtful planning preceded action and everyone's dignity was honored.

One of my professors had an extremely bad habit. During classroom discussions, when a student was trying to present an idea or ask a question, he'd often cut them off mid-sentence and give us *his* view of things. At first, the other students and I didn't really perceive this as a problem. His knowledge of the subject was vast and his speaking style almost addictive. Listening to him was such a pleasure you'd almost forget that he wasn't listening to you. But eventually we realized that we weren't getting as much as we ought to from the sessions.

Finally, three of us talked it over and came up with a simple plan: We went to the professor's office and explained the situation to him. I'm convinced that our approach was responsible for our success. We began by emphasizing our immense respect for him and made clear that we didn't think he was interrupting us on purpose, but that it was affecting us adversely. The look of embarrassment that passed over his face was awful to behold. He genuinely did not realize what he had been doing. Classroom discussions immediately improved.

—Noah B.

Note: Rankism may be invisible at first, but once identified it can often be cured by little more than the offending party's basic sense of decency.   (continued)

In the next example, students chose a different strategy—going over the head of their professor to enlist the help of others of higher rank. Again, the success of the strategy seems in large part due to the fact that everyone's dignity was honored, and thoughtful planning preceded action.

In my school, one professor stands out as the most feared writing teacher. He hates excuses. "Better never than late" is his favorite saying.

In a class last semester, he started off as tough and critical as ever. But gradually, he began criticizing students personally—rather than just critiquing their work—and rambling on about the stupidity of other professors. The class was dismayed, but because he was shielded by his prestige and position, and because he had control of his students' grades, no one dared to confront him.

Finally, a group of three students decided to speak to the department chair, who immediately arranged a meeting between the professor and a few of his peers. The faculty group first acknowledged the offending teacher's years of accomplishment and service, but then made it clear that a growing number of people found his behavior abusive. The following week, the professor apologized to his classes and his behavior improved markedly, as did his mood. Because the chair and faculty approached their colleague with respect, he responded in a positive way. They managed to get relief for the students, correct the errant professor, and strengthen the entire department.

—Adam F.

trator or target, and to provide surprising and effective outcomes. An example is the anecdote in Chapter 1 about the two men in the post office. The young man's spontaneous response immediately defused a tense situation, apparently restoring a sense of dignity to the man who felt he had been wronged. [*See Sidebar, Small Acts: The Power of "I'm Sorry," p. 6.*]

Getting Started

To get started, you can just choose one action and do it. When charting your course, consider what seems natural to you and what you

One Action Leads to Another

After reading *Somebodies and Nobodies* by Robert Fuller, Stephanie Heuer, a technology educator at an elementary school in the San Jose Unified School district, asked hundreds of students to complete the statements, "I Feel Like Nobody When..." and "I Feel Like Somebody When..." Heuer then put 50 of their responses into a book that is now being used in classrooms around the world to help young readers explore issues of dignity and respect. Entitled *Dignity Rocks!: I Feel Like Nobody When. . . I Feel Like Somebody When...*, the book is also being used to help children learn communication techniques to combat rankism in the classroom and at home.

Since then, Heuer has developed DignityRocks! seminars for children and teenagers. They are available to schools through her website, www.dignityrocks.com.

~~~

• I feel like nobody when other kids make fun of my clothes.
• I feel like nobody when I miss a goal playing soccer.
• I feel like nobody when I am ignored.
• I feel like nobody when my parents fight. It scares me.

• I feel like somebody when I help my dad outside. I like to cut the grass.
• I feel like somebody when my friends recognize what I do best.
• I feel like somebody when I get a big hug.
• I feel like somebody when I help my little sister with her homework.
• She thinks I know everything. She thinks I'm a somebody.

—From *Dignity Rocks!: I Feel Like Nobody When. . . I feel Like Somebody When...*, edited by Stephanie Heuer, illustrated by Simon Goodway, AuthorHouse, 2005.

like to do. Maybe your role is to help raise consciousness about rankism. Maybe it's to organize a million-person march on Washington. Or maybe it is to bring calm to the anger that rankism generates. If you contemplate the actions that are right for you, you're likely to have greater impact than if you try to do it someone else's way. You will probably also feel less stressed.

KEY POINTS:

- A variety of approaches are available for counteracting rankism, including interpersonal, organizational, political, psychological/ transformational, spiritual, and intuitive.

- If you choose approaches that are natural and enjoyable to you, you're likely to be more effective and experience less stress.

chapter ten

Recovering from Rankism

When people experience rankism, they typically need time to recover, especially when rankism has been chronic. They may also need to gain confidence that the perpetrators will not revert to their rankist ways. Among the most effective models for helping individuals, groups, and even entire societies recover from rankism are the Truth and Reconciliation processes used in South Africa after the end of apartheid and in Northern Ireland to aid the Protestant-Catholic peace process.

The method involves target and perpetrator sitting down together and telling the truth to each other. The perpetrator listens while the target describes in a personal way what he or she experienced at the hands of the perpetrator and the effect it had. Perpetrators acknowledge their wrongdoing. The opportunity to speak the truth and have it acknowledged is emotionally powerful and transformative because it is dignifying. It often opens the doorway to genuine forgiveness and reconciliation.

The Truth and Reconciliation model can be used by anyone, from individuals resolving differences to governments that have wronged their people. When these processes are used skillfully and compassionately, they can be freeing for all involved. (It is important to have a skilled facilitator mediating the conversations.) Effective leaders recognize that unless there are opportunities for all parties to be heard, the wounds of rankism fester and may remain unresolved for generations.

Apologies also go a long way toward helping targets of rankism to heal. The apology extended to the Aboriginal Peoples of Australia by that country's Prime Minister is one example, as is Pope Benedict XVI's apology on behalf of the Catholic Church to the victims of clergy sexual abuse.

For individuals, various healing methods can help release the emotional residue of rankism, such as anger, grief, or rage. Of special note is therapeutic work being done with forgiveness, which is recognized as a powerful agent in healing trauma and resolving conflict, from intimate relationships to international relations. Research and practice has demonstrated that forgiveness can be taught.*

You can also aid recovery from rankism by standing up to it when it occurs and/or taking action to prevent it. Helping to build a culture of dignity restores a sense of agency—the feeling that what you say and do makes a difference—and helps shift your focus from past wrongs to positive forward movement.

KEY POINTS:

- **Targets of rankism typically need time to recover from its effects.**

- **Truth and Reconciliation processes and official apologies provide models for helping individuals, groups, and societies recover from rankism.**

- **Forgiveness and other healing approaches that release the difficult emotions resulting from rankism can be taught to and used by individuals.**

- **Taking action to build a culture of dignity can also aid recovery.**

---

*See the Stanford Forgiveness Project and other forgiveness resources listed on www.dignityforall.org.

chapter eleven

Preventing Rankism

To create a dignitarian world, we need to counteract rankism when it occurs, but we also need to prevent it. This requires a proactive, rather than a reactive, stance and usually involves initiating new processes and procedures, and sometimes training, to help foster a culture of dignity. Below are some overarching principles that can serve as guidelines for thought and behavior when deliberately creating a culture of dignity, followed by some practical ways to begin building a dignitarian world.

Dignity Principles

Dignity is a basic need. It is necessary for healthy growth and development. Therefore, dignity is not optional. We must accord dignity to all.

Rankism begets rankism. The human tendency is to respond to rankism with rankism. We can stop that cycle by not responding to rankism with more rankism, and by proactively creating a climate of dignity.

Dignity works. Not only is treating others with dignity advisable on moral and humanitarian grounds, but it is practical. Businesses, organizations, and community groups that foster dignity are more productive, peaceful, and resilient than those that allow rankist behavior.

Always keep others' dignity intact. Protect others' dignity as you would your own—even those who are insulting yours. Many religious and philosophical systems advocate a standard of behavior similar to "The Golden Rule," which says, Do unto others as you would have them do unto you. That's a pretty reliable standard for determining whether what you are about to do is protecting others' dignity as you would your own.

Proactive is more effective than reactive. It is usually more effective to prevent rankism by creating a proactive plan for change, rather than by reacting to rankism when it occurs.

A paternalistic system is inherently rankist, no matter how benevolent it may be. A leadership system that does not allow people to voice their own needs, hopes, and concerns is inherently rankist because it presumes that those in power always know best what is important and necessary to others' lives, even without asking them.

Rankism creates a dysfunctional system. Rankism produces psychological, emotional, and organizational dysfunction and may stimulate a wide range of unhealthy behaviors, such as undue fear, bullying, unproductive gossip, silencing of cautionary or creative voices, cliques, bootlicking, backbiting, undermining, or sabotage. [See p. 42.] To create a healthier system, eliminate rankism.

To create "tipping point change," focus in one area until it "tips." *The Tipping Point* author Malcolm Gladwell has advised that to effectively create a tipping point, it is best to focus efforts on one relatively small area first—such as a single school, rather than the entire school district; or a single town government, rather than an entire state government—until the desired change reaches a tipping point within that smaller entity; then move to another small entity within the system, rather than trying to get a large system to "tip" all at once.

Allow everyone a voice—and listen attentively. In a culture of dignity, everyone's voice is important, even essential—not just because it's "the right thing to do," but also because it is in everyone's self-interest. When people experience rankism, if they have no effective way to respond they may seek to sabotage the organization or the perpetrators of the rankism. If we are to avoid sabotage and retaliation, we must treat others with dignity. Listening attentively minimizes sabotage.

Teach, learn—and tell others. As you gain experience creating cultures of dignity, you can teach others what you know, even as you seek to learn more. A summary of rankism and its consequences, as well as a list of additional resources, are available at www.dignityforall.org.

Building a Dignitarian World

Model building to effect change wherever you are

To proactively build a culture of dignity in your own life, we suggest using an approach we call "model building." It is regularly used by scientists and mathematicians and involves what is known as "the scientific method." Scientists start with a question or problem to be solved and then build a "model" in their minds to help them solve it. They hypothesize a solution or theory about how something works, then test it out, receive feedback, and revise their theory, until their model adequately and reliably makes sense of the data or produces a desired outcome.

The rest of us use model building too. We create ideas in our heads of how things work and then act on those ideas, receive feedback from our environment, revise our models, and act again. Architects do this when creating models of buildings to help them identify problems before actual construction occurs. Parents use model building when they try to solve problems encountered with child rearing, such as how to get their small children to go to sleep at bedtime. We all use model building in our everyday life. [*See Sidebar, Model Building in Ordinary Life.*]

To use model building to create a culture of dignity, we suggest the following steps:

1. Choose your focus (e.g. home, school, work, local government, place of worship).

2. Observe and assess the environment in terms of which aspects are rankist and which are dignitarian.

3. Formulate a model of what this system might look like if it were more dignitarian, e.g., what might you do to change it for the better and what might be some possible effects.

4. Study the environment to assess which aspects are rankist and which are dignitarian.

5. Receive and contemplate feedback. Observe the results and think about what worked well and what didn't.

6. Revise your model. Make any changes to it that you think might be helpful.

7. Try out your new model, receive feedback, and revise it again, until you get results you are happy with.

A more detailed discussion of these steps and how to use them can be found in *Resource A, Creating Your Own Plan for Change*.

Effecting Change in Organizations

What one individual or small group of people can do

One individual or small group of people can do a lot to set a tone of dignity within an organization and to institute dignitarian changes that ripple through the entire system. Some actions are surprisingly simple, such as copying all committee or board members on all e-mails, as a standard practice, to ensure that information is shared openly and equally and cliques don't develop within the organization; or focusing on how a decision is reached—in a way that ensures that multiple perspectives are heard—rather than focusing solely on reaching "the right" outcome; or consciously listening to the truth in what is being said, rather than to who is saying it. A list of practical ways to foster dignity within an organization, from a former public school board president, appears in *Resource B, Ten Ways to Foster Dignitarian Governance*.

Model Building in Ordinary Life

I learned about model building from my mother. No one called it that; it was just what you did, the way you solved problems or made decisions, the way you lived in the world. If I asked my mother why I had to do something a certain way, she never said "because I said so," or even just "because." She always had a reason for why this way worked better than others. I was free to propose a different way—a different model— if I could come up with a more useful, effective, or efficient one, based on reason, observation, experience, or insight.

Whether it was folding laundry, dealing practically with difficult (i.e., rankist) school officials, or understanding the complex psychology of human interaction, no model was static. Solutions and approaches changed and improved, and the superior model won out. I remember how her model for unloading hay bales from a wagon on our farm saved me from my own less effective approach, which had caused me considerable strain and struggle. ("I think of it as a puzzle," she said, as she gracefully selected the next bale most easily removed from the pile.)

When I was a young adult interested in child rearing, she explained to me how, periodically, she used to secretly put new books on the bookshelf for her small children to "discover" on their own. She read philosophy and psychology, using others' thinking as a springboard to develop and refine her own theories about why the people we knew acted the way they did.

It was exciting and adventurous, this way of approaching the world. No job was mundane, no chore particularly tedious. Everything was an opportunity for model building, for intellectual engagement. From my mother, I learned to observe, to contemplate, to formulate hypotheses and theories, to seek new and better solutions.

—Pamela Gerloff

Dignity Training

Another way to prevent rankism is to provide training that (a) sensitizes people to the effects of rank abuse and (b) teaches new behaviors that support dignity. Suze Rutherford and Kim Holl of International Training Associates are implementing Kindness Campaigns in schools and communities throughout the country to help prevent rankism among young people. The program allows children and teenagers to examine issues related to bullying, harassment, cliques, common meanness, and other forms of rankism. Using the arts, conversation, and play, participants are invited to look beyond labels and to treat each other with dignity. [*See Resource C, Stories of Dignity Regained, resulting from Kindness Campaigns in schools. See also www.dignityforall.org for information about various dignity training programs.*]

Collaborative Leadership

Collaborative leadership is inherently more dignitarian than are authoritarian governance styles because a collaborative model seeks to listen to, respect, and value the contributions of an entire community. Collaborative approaches typically take more time when designing policies and making important decisions, but they are more likely to secure buy-in and compliance, as well as feelings of enthusiasm and loyalty, from different constituent groups.

A collaborative, shared-leadership process was used by Miss Hall's School, a college preparatory, all-girls boarding school in the northeastern United States, to design a cell phone policy for students. A student-led initiative to change the school's cell phone policy was begun, with the aim of developing a policy that would preserve the culture of respect and dignity to which the school has long been committed. Over a two-year period, students led the school community in an Appreciative Inquiry Process focusing on what members of the community wanted to preserve as they anticipated change. All voices were heard. Students, teachers, and staff shared stories related to the schools' core values. The result was a new policy that appealed to all. [*See Sidebar for information about the Appreciative Inquiry Process at Miss Hall's School.*]

Establishing system-wide change

When key figures in an organization decide to create a culture of dignity, the resulting changes can enhance the lives of everyone. An important ingredient for success is collaborative processes that involve all stakeholder groups. During the 1960s in the United States, system-wide processes to make institutions less sexist demonstrated that sexism could be significantly reduced. These can serve as models for making institutions of today less rankist. System-wide efforts to reduce rankism may include such elements as

- special committees and open hearings to investigate rankism and to recommend new policies to safeguard dignity;

Appreciative Inquiry to Support a Culture of Dignity

The online encyclopedia *Wikipedia* defines Appreciative Inquiry as "a particular way of asking questions and envisioning the future that fosters positive relationships and builds on the basic goodness in a person, a situation, or an organization. In so doing, it enhances a system's capacity for collaboration and change.... The basic idea is to build organizations around what works, rather than trying to fix what doesn't." (http://en.wikipedia.org/wiki/Appreciative Inquiry)

Below are some of the Appreciative Inquiry questions students asked members of the Miss Hall's School community to prompt them to share their experiences and reflections, as part of a student-led initiative to change the school's cell phone policy in a way that would preserve its culture of respect and dignity. The questions are based on the school's core values of growth, honor, authenticity, and respect.

1. Since you've been part of Miss Hall's School, can you describe the ways in which you have grown?

2. Can you talk about someone in the community (student, faculty, or staff member) whom you would describe as authentic?

3. What is the most honorable thing that you have ever seen someone in this community do?

4. Can you talk about a time when you were treated with respect in this community?

- a truth and reconciliation process like the one used in South Africa to help heal the wounds of apartheid, but focused on healing the wounds of rankism;

- shared evaluation processes for employees at all levels;

- creation of an ombudsperson position or ombudscommittee;

- periodic institutional reviews to evaluate the organizational climate with regard to rankism and dignity;

- ongoing, open discussion of issues of rankism and dignity.

The above strategies for establishing system-wide change are discussed further in *Resource D, How to Create a Culture of Dignity.*

Top-down Change at the National Level

Building a dignitarian world can take surprising turns. One example is the Southeast Asian kingdom of Bhutan's transition, over the past decade, from an absolute monarchy to a constitutional monarchy, and, ultimately, to a parliamentary democracy. It's surprising because it happened from the top down.

Historically, the transition from an autocracy to a democracy has typically occurred through some element of force, with the nation's people coming to see themselves as capable of claiming initiative and power. However, key leaders among a nation's royalty have sometimes exerted a moral force that encouraged their subjects to assume the responsibilities of self-government. Spain's king, Juan Carlos, facilitated his country's transition to democratic government after decades of authoritarian rule, even intervening to quash a reactionary coup. Similarly, Bhutan's King Jigme Singye Wangchuck initiated the process that gradually handed over power to the people by giving executive authority to a cabinet of ministers and ordering a new democratic constitution to be drafted. In 2008, general elections signaled Bhutan's transition to a parliamentary democracy.

KEY POINTS:

- Preventing rankism requires a proactive approach.

- Following the ten dignity principles can help guide our thoughts and actions when creating a dignitarian culture.

- A model building approach enables each of us as individuals to effect dignitarian changes wherever we are.

- Individuals and small groups can have large impact on organizational systems through their attitudes and behaviors.

- System-wide change is supported through collaborative processes that involve all stakeholder groups and respect the dignity of individuals.

- When key leaders at the top of a hierarchy are committed to dignity, surprising things can happen.

chapter twelve

Building a Dignitarian World

We believe that building a dignitarian society is democracy's next natural evolutionary step. Dignity for all is a stepping stone to realizing the democratic promise of liberty and justice for all. And yet, dignity is not only for democracies. While democracies provide individuals with unprecedented freedom to actively help create a dignitarian culture, dignity is a universal need and people everywhere require it to thrive. And so, wise leaders in any governmental system will seek ways to use their rank to respect and protect the dignity of the citizenry; and compassionate and courageous individuals everywhere—regardless of their country's political traditions and institutions—will seek ways to bring greater dignity to everyone.

As individuals, we have the power to claim dignity for ourselves, to grant it to others, and to stand up for the principle of dignity for all. We can make a decision to act on the understanding that dignity is so fundamental to the flourishing of the human spirit that *dignity is not optional*. Rather, dignity is the foundation of all human relations.

Since dignity matters, and it matters to everyone, then isn't it time to ask, *What would it take to build a dignitarian world*—and together, live the answer?

Creating Your Own Plan for Change

As an individual, you can help create a world without rankism, whether you choose to focus on creating a culture of dignity at home, school, work, within a social group or recreational activity, your house of worship, or your local or global community. Here are some ideas to help you create your own plan of action.

Reinterpret Rank as Role

When targeting or preventing rankism, it can be useful to first change our own ways of thinking about rank. One example of how to do this is to reconceptualize rank as role, instead of thinking of it as a hierarchy in which people of high rank have greater power than others and therefore have more status and are more "important." Looking at rank as role, you can think of everyone as characters in a play.

Each has been cast in a role. Some roles have wider spheres of responsibility than others; some have greater decision-making authority; some wield greater power; some appear to have higher status. But all roles are needed—the high-ranking as well as the low. Without every single role the play would not be complete.

Similarly, in "real life," individuals whose roles may appear small or unimportant, or who question the abuse of power inherent in rank—such as an angry dissenter, a family's "black sheep" child, or an organizational system's group of blacklisted "troublemakers"—would not be dismissed or devalued if viewed as characters in a play. In any play, antagonists are as essential as protagonists and so are characters with seemingly small or "unimportant" roles. Even someone with an apparently inconsequential—or distasteful—part contributes something vital to the play. And in the next play, the characters' roles may be shuffled around: The lead in the previous play may not play the lead in the next one; identities shift; roles change—just as in "real life."

When we reconceptualize rank as role, we are less apt to abuse our own rank because we can readily recognize that the power and perks rank may carry do not confer any lasting importance or specialness. Every individual, regardless of rank, is merely playing a needed, temporary role.

Breaking out of our habitual ways of thinking by perceiving rank as role is a powerful step toward preventing rankism. It also supports dignity for all by allowing more people to step into positions of leadership and offer their contributions. Over time, as people learn to listen to one another from the vantage point of different roles, empathy for and understanding of others' experiences tend to naturally occur.

Imagine New Ways of Fostering and Honoring Dignity

We all have ideas, images, or models in our heads of how things work, what we expect in the world, and how to respond to different types of experience. These ideas—many of which are developed in childhood—guide us in determining our own behavior. To prevent abuse of rank before it occurs, it can be useful to imagine new images of what a culture of dignity might look like in different contexts and how we might create such cultures.

Create Models and Test Them

Scientists create models of the human body or the Earth's ecosystem to better understand how the physical world operates. Psychologists create models of the human mind and emotions in order to help people develop more optimal behaviors. All of us, in daily life, create models in our heads that aid us in solving problems and interacting with our world.

Our models and images constantly evolve and change, as we first formulate an idea or hypothesis, then test it out, and subsequently observe and assess the results; we then revise our hypotheses and theories, based on our observations. In this way, we continually update our models to make them more useful, accurate, or predictive. To bring about specific results, we continue to refine them until they are able to produce in "the real world" the kinds of results we imagine in our minds.

Invent Dignitarian Models

Most of our current models for human functioning are not dignitarian. Rankism is an accepted element of the ways we habitually think about living together, from family life to international relations. To create a dignitarian world—one in which dignity becomes the natural and expected experience—we can examine our models of relationship to determine whether they are enabling the creation of a dignitarian world. Then we can invent new models that facilitate the experience of dignity for all. Below is a step-by-step process for doing this. It is intended as an example only and may be altered as appropriate for your needs.

1. Choose Your Focus

Begin with the intention to create a model that will foster dignity for all. Then choose an area on which to focus (e.g., family, school, spiritual community, work, or local, state, or national government).

2. Observe and Assess

Now, observe how this system you are involved in functions, in terms of dignity and rankism. Some questions to ask might be:

Do people feel they are valued as individuals?

Do they experience that their unique contributions are recognized and welcomed?

Do people have ways to communicate both their vision for the group or organization as a whole and their concerns about the functioning of the overall system?

Is the system functioning harmoniously and productively?

Do people feel stressed, anxious, angry, or depressed?

Are people able to express their views, or are some voices silenced?

Do leaders and other group members seem to respect one another?

Does any bullying or intimidation occur?

Is the system "open" or "closed" in terms of allowing everyone to be involved?

Do you need to be a member of a clique or "special network" to have full access to rights and privileges of the group?

These are some initial questions you can ask in order to get a sense of the degree of dignity being fostered in the culture you are looking at. If your position in the organizational system permits, you may be able to distribute a questionnaire with questions such as these, to help in your assessment. You may want to see if you can identify mechanisms in the organization that support dignity and ones that undermine it.

3. Formulate a Model

a. Based on your observations, begin to formulate a model of what this system might look like if it were to implement mechanisms to support dignity for all.

What kinds of processes and procedures might help create a culture of dignity?
What could people in high-ranking positions do to help create such a culture?
What could people in lower ranking positions do?
What could you do?

For instance, you might think about what could be done to ensure that everyone has a chance to give input about decisions before they occur. You might consider ways to make decision-making more open and information about important matters available to everyone, so that a climate of secrecy does not develop. If people in your organization or community feel at risk when they bring up concerns about rankism, you might designate a neutral person to serve as ombudsperson to help investigate and mediate complaints.

b. As you build your models, beware of the pitfalls of wallowing in process! This is the point where you will begin to shift from focusing on process to outcome. While it is important to eliminate abuses of rank in the best possible ways, it is also very important to streamline decision making and reach a timely decision. You may need to accept that some of your decisions will be wrong, or less than ideal, but it is nonetheless best to go ahead in a timely fashion. Sometimes you can find out what needs to be changed only by taking action and correcting course.

4. Try Out Your Model

Now, try out your model in any way that seems practical. You might first imagine it only in your mind. If this person or governing body were to do this, what might be the result? If this person or group were to do that, what might happen? If you were to do such and such, what might follow? Identify potential problems and try to come up with ways to prevent or resolve them. For example, if you want to propose the creation of an ombudsperson position, you might think about the best way to suggest the idea, so as to avoid its rejection and maximize its chances of adoption. Who in the organization is likely to be most receptive to the idea? Who would be in the best position to bring the idea to the appropriate decision-makers?

You could also ask a friend, colleague, or small group of others to help you think this through. Other viewpoints are often helpful because they multiply the perspectives through which you can look at your model. As noted above, you don't need to overdo the input process. Seek enough input to give additional perspective, but not so much that you get bogged down.

Once your model or idea is ready to be tested, find ways to implement portions of it on a small scale. To do that within an organization, it is sometimes easiest to enlist the aid of people in positions of relatively high rank, if you are not in such a position yourself. If that's not possible, do what you can from where you are.

5. Receive and Contemplate Feedback

As you try out aspects of your model, observe the results. It's best to record them, so you don't lose important information. (Memory usually fades over time.) Actively solicit feedback from others: Ask them to describe their experiences. Are the new procedures helping them to feel more valued, listened to, or heard? Do they feel the environment has become safer for people to express a diversity of views? Do they feel less stress or anxiety than before? Ask questions that will help you determine the effectiveness of the model you have been trying out.

6. Revise Your Model

Based on the feedback you have collected, identify what seems to be working well, what isn't, what you think should stay the same, and what you would like to revise in your model. Make your revisions.

7. Keep Revising and Testing Your Model

Try out your new model, receive feedback, and revise it again, until you get results you are happy with. In this way, over time, you can help build a dignitarian culture, whatever your position or rank, in whatever sphere you choose to work in.

Ten Ways to Foster Dignitarian Governance

By Brian J. Gerloff

It's not uncommon for governing boards to engage in rankism, often unintentionally. For example, board members may assume they have superior knowledge and therefore disregard the views of their constituency. Within the board itself, members may assume the majority is wiser than the minority. Rankism can also occur in the ranks of the organization if board members fail to hold administrators to dignitarian standards of behavior. Some ways boards can reduce rankism in their organization include:

1. Remember that everyone on the board has equal legitimacy.

This means that you must *listen to all the varying perspectives on a board* as you make decisions. Of course you should look for common ground when possible, but it also means that *sometimes you will not have unanimous votes*. You won't always have consensus decisions if you are genuinely allowing everyone's voice to be heard and considered.

2. Share information equally with all board members.

When information is provided to one member of the board, make it standard practice to provide it to all, e.g., by forwarding informational e-mails to everyone and by copying all members of a committee with all correspondence. This promotes a culture of equality on the board and prevents the formation of cliques.

3. Don't assign the same seats for every meeting.

Rotating seating helps establish a norm of everyone relating to everyone, not just to certain individuals.

4. Remember that the board acts on behalf of the larger organization.

If you are on a school board, you represent the entire community. If you are on a church council, you represent the entire congregation. While it is right for you to have access to more information than your constituents, and while it's true that you may sometimes have a clearer perspective on a situation than someone who is less involved, you nonetheless have a responsibility to include, involve, and listen to your constituents. Focus groups, surveys, constituent committees, and open discussion forums can help you stay in touch with the wishes and per- spectives of the people you are representing.

5. Listen to the truth in what is being said, regardless of who is saying it.

A nugget of truth may come from anyone, including those who may not appear polished, articulate, or highly educated. Listening for the truth behind the appearance affords everyone the dignity they deserve—and also results in better decision making.

6. Set dignitarian standards of conduct for administrators, executives, and board members, requiring them to treat employees and stakeholders with respect—and establish methods to monitor that.

Client and constituent surveys and an office of ombudsperson are some effective ways to monitor performance.

7. Think of yourself as a servant-leader.

If the concept of servant leadership informs your role as a board mem- ber, it tends to change the way you look at your responsibilities. Service becomes the primary organizing principle.

8. Think "governance," not "management"—and use a dignitarian model.

The role of a board is to govern, not manage. The Carver governance model identifies policies and practices that help establish both a high-performing board and high-performing administrators, while maintaining high standards of integrity, purpose, and respect. [*See* *www.carvergovernance.com* and Boards That Make a Difference: A New Design for Leadership in Nonprofit and Public Organizations *(Jossey-Bass, 1990; 3rd edition, 2006)*].

9. Be concerned about "how" a decision is reached—not just about reaching the "right" decision.

Difficult decisions that are reached by listening, considering, and perhaps compromising are more likely to be strongly supported by an organization than when the "right" decision is imposed without carefully considering alternative perspectives and points of view.

10. Leave a lasting legacy.

A board committed to inclusive and dignitarian leadership can positively influence the community it serves well into the future, even after individual board members have come and gone. Here's an example from the school district on whose board I served: A public referendum was recently passed harmoniously and enthusiastically. Rather than the school board or staff formulating a plan for the rapid growth expected in the school population, the district underwent a long information-gathering process. It included an 80-member committee of citizens, which developed a plan and sought feedback via written surveys and a full year of open houses. The success of the referendum and, more importantly, the inclusive and respectful process used, are examples of what can happen when boards insist on dignity for all. Making a dignitarian approach to governance standard operating procedure allows a dignitarian ethic to take hold in the culture and produce positive effects for years to come.

Dr. Brian Gerloff is a practicing large-animal veterinarian. He served on the board of a public school district in Illinois for eight years, six of them as president. At the close of his years of service, the Illinois State Board of Education honored him with its "Education Hero" award, in recognition of his contributions to public education in the state of Illinois.

Stories of Dignity Regained

By Suze Rutherford and Kim Holl

To help build a dignitarian world, International Training Associates is implementing Kindness Campaigns in schools and communities throughout the United States. These help young people recognize rankism and its effects on themselves and others. Through creative play, the arts, and deep conversation, participants learn to look beyond labels and to treat each other with dignity.

Story 1: During one of our Middle School Respect Days, our attention was drawn to a quiet, morose, overweight eighth-grade boy who in his invisibility was obviously at the lower end of the social hierarchy. He had difficulty participating in the activities until we were writing a group poem in which each student wrote a line. After all his peers had shared, this young man found his voice and quietly stood up and read "In a kind world, girls would like me." There was an audible gasp and many students cried as they were touched by his naked honesty and pain. Although they had gone to school together since kindergarten, this was the first time many truly saw his humanity. This was the beginning of a transformation where others began to treat him with dignity and he himself began to find his voice and see himself as worthwhile.

Story 2: The coach of a high school girls' volleyball team noticed that the girls on her team were participating in ruthless relational aggression antics with each other and other girls at the school. These girls were at the top of the social hierarchy. They abused their power to maintain their status and in the wake caused such damage that several girls transferred schools to maintain their dignity. International Training Associates was invited in to intervene. Through deep conversation about rankism, the girls began to realize that with the power of privilege comes huge responsibility to treat others with dignity. By enlisting the girls to use their leadership skills in a prosocial way as members of a Youth Action Council, they invited girls from five other schools to participate in local, national, and global service initiatives. They became involved in something bigger than themselves by mentoring younger girls and raising money to send six girls in Tanzania to school for one year. Their behavior towards their peers changed once they had realized the impact of their abuse of power and rank. They healed themselves through their acts of kindness.

For more information about the Kindness Campaign, visit www.trainingweal.org.

How to Create a Culture of Dignity

(Excerpted and adapted from *All Rise: Somebodies, Nobodies, and the Politics of Dignity* by Robert W. Fuller, Berrett-Koehler: San Francisco, 2006.)

The Need for Collaboration

It's impossible to know exactly what a particular dignitarian institution will look like in advance, because to qualify as dignitarian its design must take into account the views of those the institution will serve. In a dignitarian organization, everyone involved has a voice and everyone's views have some political weight. *The most important element in creating a dignitarian organization is to design a process that is collaborative and involves all stakeholders.* (Leaders often design programs without involving the people they serve, and that's one reason their ideas so often fall flat. Not only is such an approach ineffective, it is also rankist, because it assumes that the leaders necessarily know what would be best for an organization and the people it is meant to serve.)

Therefore, a template can only suggest an approach and basic framework for transforming an organization into a dignitarian one.

Suggested Components

As a basic model, a process used by many academic institutions in the 1960s to make institutions less sexist can serve as a template for making institutions of today less rankist.

1. Shared Governance: Using Special Committees and Open Hearings

During the 1960s, many academic institutions established special committees on the status of women. Typically, these committees were composed of women administrators, faculty, students, alumni, and staff, and also included a few men. They held open hearings on campus, during which anyone could call attention to policies or practices that were felt to demean women or put them at a disadvantage. The committees then compiled a list of specific instances of unfairness or abuse, along with potential remedies, and presented it to the administrator, group, or governing body with the power to redress the grievances at issue. Their final task was to persuade that official or body to adopt the recommended changes.

Similarly, as we build more dignitarian institutions, special committees to investigate the status of persons (specifically with regard to dignity) can be established. Open hearings can allow participants to point out ways in which members of various constituencies feel their dignity is not respected. A portion of the complaints may be contested, and some may eventually be judged to be unfounded. A number of the valid ones will be relatively easy to address. Other problems may take years or even decades to correct.

Key Elements of the Committee Approach

a. High-level Participation

The likelihood of success using committees and open hearings is greatly enhanced by the involvement of a figure of very high rank in the organization who makes it clear that it is safe for others to seriously challenge the status quo. It need not be the president, but, if not, it must be someone whom everyone knows speaks for the president.

b. Fixed Deadlines

Second, each committee must have a fixed deadline against which it works. As the postwar British Prime Minister Clement Atlee noted, "Democracy means government by discussion, but it is only effective if you can stop people talking."

c. Everyone Has a Voice

Dignitarian governance does not necessarily mean giving everyone a vote on every issue, but it does mean giving everyone a voice. To ensure those voices are heard usually requires having at least some voting representatives from each of the organization's various constituencies serving at every level of its governance. This is sometimes referred to as multi-stake-holder or collaborative problem-solving.

For example, in an academic institution this means adding students and alumni to committees on student life, educational policy, and appointments and promotions; to the governing faculty body itself; and also to the board of trustees. Typically, such representatives hold 5-15 percent of the seats, but the percentage could go higher. The aim is to ensure that every group has an opportunity to make its interests known. This goal is given teeth by providing each group with enough votes to determine the outcome in situations when the group as a whole is closely divided. Vote ratios between various constituencies mirror their relative degree of responsibility for achieving each specific goal of the institution. Thus, students would have a decisive majority of votes on a student life committee; faculty a decisive majority on educational policy. And students, faculty, and administrators would all play minority roles in fiduciary decisions that traditionally are decided by the board of trustees.

Including voting representatives from all constituencies creates an environment in which the authorities do not merely deign to listen to those of lower rank. Rather, it behooves them to treat everyone with dignity because at the end of the day everyone will be exercising some degree of voting power over the outcome.

2. Shared Evaluation Process

In addition to shared governance, a dignitarian institution is likely to possess a number of other distinctive characteristics. For example, the evaluation process would be broadened so that people from constituencies other than the one for which the person is being evaluated would be involved in hiring decisions and reviews of job performance. In the corporate world, such evaluation models are referred to as "360-degree reviews." All comments are provided as feedback to the employee.

3. Ombudsperson or Committee
Another useful practice is the appointment of an ombudsperson with broad responsibility for resolving disputes over the use and abuse of rank, or a committee with similar powers. Princeton University's ombudsman in 2004, Camilo Azcarate, said that his job can largely be summed up as making the distinction between rank and rankism in a wide variety of circumstances. Whether an individual or a larger body, it is essential that organizations have a neutral party to whom individuals can go without fear of reprisal to help resolve issues of indignity.

4. Ongoing Institutional Reviews
Additionally, institution-wide constitutional reviews could be scheduled—every five or ten years—to update the system of governance in light of changing circumstances, to ensure that it remains dignitarian.

5. Truth and Reconciliation Process
Although often challenging to implement, a Truth and Reconciliation process similar to those used in Ireland and South Africa [see pp. 59-60] can be carried out on a smaller scale within organizations, and may sometimes be necessary. A process by which individuals and groups who feel they have been treated in a rankist way can meet with those they feel have wronged them, for the purpose of mutual understanding and reconciliation, can heal past hurts and help prevent rankism in the future.

6. Open Discussion
Because rankism thrives in a climate of secrecy and silencing, implementing any or all of the above practices will naturally decrease the levels of rankism in an organization because the silence around rankism will have been broken. Once people are genuinely allowed to talk about it, rankism begins to lose its grip.

About the Authors

Robert W. Fuller, Ph.D., former president of Oberlin College, is an internationally recognized authority on the subject of rankism and dignity. His books and ideas have been widely covered in the media, including *The New York Times, Oprah Magazine*, National Public Radio, C-SPAN, *The Boston Globe*, the BBC and *Voice of America*. Fuller has given more than 300 talks at a variety of organizations, from Princeton University to Microsoft to Kaiser Hospital. He may be reached at fuller@dignityforall.org.

Pamela A. Gerloff, Ed.D., is the founder of Compelling Vision, a consulting business whose clients have included Procter & Gamble, the University of Massachusetts, and the U.S. Army. She currently writes for a diverse audience and provides presentations, training, and consulting to individuals and organizations seeking to create dignitarian environments. Her unique approach to change grew out of two fundamental questions she began to ask herself while pursuing a doctorate in Human Development at Harvard University's Graduate School of Education: *Why doesn't change last?* and *Why does it seem so hard?* Her surprising findings led her to focus on effecting deep-level, lasting change with grace, gentleness, and ease. She may be reached at gerloff@dignityforall.org.

For more information about the authors and their work, please visit www.dignityforall.org.

www.dignityforall.org

The ultimate purpose of this book is to help spread the dignity meme.

Meme (pronounced *meem*)

> *n. a cultural unit (an idea or value or pattern of behavior) that is passed from one person to another by non-genetic means (as by imitation); "memes are the cultural counterpart of genes"**

It is already happening. From the United States to India to China, to Korea, Canada, the United Kingdom, France, Australia, South Africa, New Zealand—on every continent—people are embracing the big idea contained in this little book. **Dignity is an idea whose time has come.**

In the United States, a government worker in a major city has begun programs to provide support, education, and tools for employees affected by rankism.

In Canada, a labor union is proposing to make a rankism-free workplace a goal of contract negotiations.

In India, dignitarian values are emerging as a clear alternative to the residual influence of the traditional caste system.

In schools throughout the USA, programs to end bullying are being implemented.

In the United Kingdom, the BBC World Service has broadcast programming about dignity and rankism.

In politics, dignity for all is one of those rare ideas on which both liberals and conservatives can agree, and some leaders are using it to find common ground.

---

*Dictionary.com. WordNet® 3.0. Princeton University. http://dictionary.reference.com/browse/meme (accessed: April 30, 2008)

In major corporations, equal dignity regardless of rank is beginning to be seen as promoting creativity, productivity, company loyalty, and personal well-being.

In healthcare, the concept of rankism is being applied to the reform of nursing education.

In homes and families, the idea that "kids are people too" is becoming self-evident.

To learn more, come to www.dignityforall.org.

We offer:

E-newsletter keeping you up-to-date on where and how the dignity meme is spreading

Tip sheets to help you counteract rankism and bring more dignity into your world

Resource list of books, websites, and articles of interest

Interview archives, including some of Robert Fuller's articles and interviews introducing the concept of rankism

Dignity training, coaching, and consulting services

A global community of others who value dignity

Please send us *your* experiences and ideas. We want to hear your stories of dignity, rankism, and especially, dignity regained.

www.dignityforall.org

"Congratulations on starting an absolutely crucial meme."
— *Wes Boyd,* co-founder of MoveOn.org

About Berrett-Koehler Publishers

Berrett-Koehler is an independent publisher dedicated to an ambitious mission: Creating a World That Works for All.

We believe that to truly create a better world, action is needed at all levels—individual, organizational, and societal. At the individual level, our publications help people align their lives with their values and with their aspirations for a better world. At the organizational level, our publications promote progressive leadership and management practices, socially responsible approaches to business, and humane and effective organizations. At the societal level, our publications advance social and economic justice, shared prosperity, sustainability, and new solutions to national and global issues.

A major theme of our publications is "Opening Up New Space." They challenge conventional thinking, introduce new ideas, and foster positive change. Their common quest is changing the underlying beliefs, mindsets, and structures that keep generating the same cycles of problems, no matter who our leaders are or what improvement programs we adopt.

We strive to practice what we preach—to operate our publishing company in line with the ideas in our books. At the core of our approach is *stewardship*, which we define as a deep sense of responsibility to administer the company for the benefit of all of our "stakeholder" groups: authors, customers, employees, investors, service providers, and the communities and environment around us.

We are grateful to the thousands of readers, authors, and other friends of the company who consider themselves to be part of the "BK Community." We hope that you, too, will join us in our mission.

A BK Currents Book

This book is part of our BK Currents series. BK Currents books advance social and economic justice by exploring the critical intersections between business and society. Offering a unique combination of thoughtful analysis and progressive alternatives, BK Currents books promote positive change at the national and global levels. To find out more, visit www.bkcurrents.com.

Be Connected

Visit Our Website

Go to www.bkconnection.com to read exclusive previews and excerpts of new books, find detailed information on all Berrett-Koehler titles and authors, browse subject-area libraries of books, and get special discounts.

Subscribe to Our Free E-Newsletter

Be the first to hear about new publications, special discount offers, exclusive articles, news about bestsellers, and more! Get on the list for our free e-newsletter by going to www.bkconnection.com.

Get Quantity Discounts

Berrett-Koehler books are available at quantity discounts for orders of ten or more copies. Please call us toll-free at (800) 929-2929 or email us at bkp.orders@aidcvt.com.

Host a Reading Group

For tips on how to form and carry on a book reading group in your workplace or community, see our website at www.bkconnection.com.

Join the BK Community

Thousands of readers of our books have become part of the "BK Community" by participating in events featuring our authors, reviewing draft manuscripts of forthcoming books, spreading the word about their favorite books, and supporting our publishing program in other ways. If you would like to join the BK Community, please contact us at bkcommunity@bkpub.com.

Printed in the United States
136874LV00001B/227/P